Penguin Critical Studies

Rosencrantz and
Guildenstern are Dead

Dr Roger Sales is a lecturer in the School of English and American
Studies at the University of East Anglia. He was formerly a research
assistant with B B C T V and has edited two volumes of *Shakespeare in
Perspective* (1982, 1985), which contain television and radio talks on all
of Shakespeare's plays. His other publications include *English Literature in History 1780–1830: Pastoral and Politics* (1983), which is based
on his Cambridge Ph.D. thesis and the Critical Studies volume on
Much Ado About Nothing (1987).

Penguin Critical Studies
Joint Advisory Editors:
Stephen Coote and Bryan Loughrey

Tom Stoppard

Rosencrantz and Guildenstern are Dead

Roger Sales

Penguin Books

PENGUIN BOOKS

Published by the Penguin Group
27 Wrights Lane, London W8 5TZ, England
Viking Penguin Inc., 40 West 23rd Street, New York, New York 10010, USA
Penguin Books Australia Ltd, Ringwood, Victoria, Australia
Penguin Books Canada Ltd, 2801 John Street, Markham, Ontario, Canada L3R 1B4
Penguin Books (NZ) Ltd, 182–190 Wairau Road, Auckland 10, New Zealand

Penguin Books Ltd, Registered Offices: Harmondsworth, Middlesex, England

First published 1988

Extracts reprinted by permission of Faber and Faber Ltd from *Rosencrantz and Guildenstern are
Dead, Lord Malquist and Mr Moon, The Real Inspector Hound* and
Dogg's Hamlet, Cahoot's Macbeth by Tom Stoppard

Made and printed in Great Britain by
Richard Clay Ltd, Bungay, Suffolk

Filmset in 9/11 Monophoto Times

For Anne

Contents

Critical Studies: Rosencrantz and Guildenstern are Dead

Acknowledgements

My thanks are due once again to Stephen Coote and Bryan Loughrey, the Advisory Editors for this series. Although I have always enjoyed seeing or reading Tom Stoppard's plays, it needed a suggestion from them for me to think in terms of writing this book. Mary Omond, the copy-editor at Penguin Books, suggested a number of important revisions to my original manuscript. I am also grateful to the University of East Anglia for letting me take a term of study leave in order to finish this manuscript. The staff of the University Library helped me in a number of ways, particularly by obtaining material through the inter-library loan system. I have worked at East Anglia for a number of years in close contact with a group of English Studies teachers, which includes Literature, Drama, History, Film and Linguistics specialists. I owe them, and our students, a great debt for creating an academic environment which is both challenging and supportive. Before joining this group, I worked with Raymond Williams whose approach to the study of literature still continues to influence my own. Finally, I must acknowledge two more personal debts. The first is to my parents, who introduced me to the theatre, and the second is to Anne, to whom this book is dedicated with love.

Textual Note

All quotations from *Rosencrantz and Guildenstern are Dead* are taken from the current (1986) reprint of the revised edition (December 1967). My preference is in fact for the earlier version (May 1967) not just because it contains some unbelievably corny jokes, but also because its ending puts a greater emphasis on the play's cyclical, theatrical patterns. The quotations from *Lord Malquist and Mr Moon*, *The Real Inspector Hound*, *Travesties* and *Dogg's Hamlet, Cahoot's Macbeth* are also taken from the currently available Faber and Faber editions. I have used the New Penguin Shakespeare edition of *Hamlet* and, as indicated in the Bibliography, would like to recommend Anne Barton's Introduction to students.

The quotations from Stoppard are followed by a page number. I have very occasionally omitted stage directions from them if they do not have a direct bearing on the point that is being illustrated. The quotations from Shakespeare are followed by a reference to the act, scene and line. I have used the convention by which a quotation from Act One, Scene One, lines one to seven is rendered as I.1.1–7. The quotations from other texts are taken from what are considered to be the standard editions of them. I have, where appropriate, abbreviated titles. *Rosencrantz and Guildenstern are Dead* is, for instance, shortened to *Rosencrantz*. I use Stoppard's own abbreviations of Ros and Guil to refer to the play's main characters. It should, therefore, be easy to differentiate between Stoppard's attendant lords and Shakespeare's ones, who are referred to as Rosencrantz and Guildenstern. The Bibliography lists some of the books and articles which have influenced my own readings of Stoppard. It serves a dual function in that it makes suggestions for further reading as well as acknowledging some of my own particular, and more specialized, debts. I refer during the argument itself to the interpretations of individual critics when it seems appropriate to do so, although I have chosen not to use footnotes to support such references. I wanted to make my analysis, and more importantly Stoppard's work, as accessible as possible to readers. I have made every effort, however, to ensure that the Bibliography lists the relevant sources. For example, I found Terence Hawkes's comment that a performance of *Hamlet* has 'always already begun' before the audience gets to the theatre an extremely helpful one when thinking about relationships between *Rosencrantz* and *Hamlet*. I therefore refer to it explicitly at the beginning of my own argument, as well as more implicitly throughout. The Bibliography cites the collection of essays in which Hawkes makes this remark. I have also used the Bibliography as an opportunity to draw attention to, through occasional descriptive notes, the importance of the work that has been done by individual critics whom I do not mention by name during the course of my own argument. All this means that the Bibliography itself might be rather cumbersome, although this is a risk worth running if it means that the analysis is more accessible. I have been influenced in my readings of Stoppard, either positively or negatively, by all the works cited in the Bibliography.

Much of the research for this book was done in 1985 and the earlier part of 1986. The Bibliography lists some of the studies of Stoppard which have been published since then. I have not updated my material on film, television and radio which, as argued in more detail later on, I regard as an essential context for Stoppard's plays.

Introduction

The analysis is divided into three parts. The first one offers a detailed reading of *Rosencrantz* itself. A chapter is devoted to each of its three acts. Stoppard's text does not include scene divisions. The sub-headings within these chapters nevertheless correspond to my sense of where such divisions might come. Page references are given to indicate which particular part of the text will be considered under each of these sub-headings. It is therefore possible to refer to the discussion of a particular scene without necessarily following the argument as a whole. Two important points should be remembered, however, if this approach is being adopted. First of all, more space is given to the opening scene than to any of the succeeding ones. Indeed, the first chapter as a whole establishes a general framework which can then be assumed rather than proved later on. Secondly, and following on from this, the argument inevitably accumulates its own particular terms and terms of cross-reference. In other words, it develops its own shorthand which, if encountered in isolated segments rather than within the overall flow of the argument, might sometimes prove to be a confusing one. My suggestion is that, initially, this reading of the play ought to be treated as a whole. Its structure nevertheless allows for the kind of random sampling which is often an important part of the revision process.

The second part of the analysis is much shorter and consists of a single chapter on *Hamlet*. It explores differences between Stoppard's play and Shakespeare's one, but also considers some of the similarities which other critics have tended to overlook. The emphasis is interpretative rather than purely descriptive, although the argument is established through a broadly sequential reading of the play. It may, therefore, fulfil a secondary function by offering an introduction to the play.

The third part of the analysis is a more detailed one. It sets *Rosencrantz* within the context of a limited number of Stoppard's other works. There are three chapters. The first two contain reasonably detailed textual readings, which are interspersed with sections that raise wider contextual and theoretical issues. The third one concentrates more on textual analysis, partly for reasons of space and partly because contexts for Stoppard's adaptations from Shakespeare have already been established at some length earlier on.

The thinking behind this three-part structure requires some preliminary comments, as much to justify its omissions as its inclusions. My impressions of both reviews and critical analyses of *Rosencrantz*, particularly those written during the 1960s, were not very favourable ones. They tended to be weighed down by lists of the playwrights and philosophers by whom Stoppard was supposed to have been influenced. There was a polarization between critics who asserted that he was a worthy member of this club and those who claimed that he was just a plagiarist and a parasite. Both these positions represent an inadequate, and rather naïve, response to parody. It is, of course, much easier to recognize Stoppard as a parodist now that it is possible to set *Rosencrantz* within the context of his later works. I would still maintain, however, that the internal textual evidence is overwhelming and that it was either missed, or misinterpreted, by most of Stoppard's early critics.

Versions of this initial polarization of critical opinion are still to be found in more recent studies. Some critics praise Stoppard for including a lot of philosophical and metaphysical speculations, which prove that he is a serious artist. Others claim that he is not metaphysical enough, or else that he treats such serious matters too frivolously. Such positions remain trapped within the narrow confines of an arid debate. Irving Wardle claimed back in 1968, in a review wittily if mistakenly entitled 'A Grin without a Cat', that Stoppard was an essentially bookish playwright. His particular complaint was that intellectual games, or the grin, were divorced from reality in the shape of the cat. The spectre of Stoppard the bookish, or academic, playwright continues to haunt responses to his plays. A number of more perceptive critics have, however, revealed that such a representation tells us more about criticism itself than it does about Stoppard's plays. Jim Hunter is right to argue that, although Stoppard may play with what appear to be weighty speculations, 'his claim on our attention is not as a thinker but as a player'. The point that surprised me most about the earlier critical responses to *Rosencrantz* was that relatively little attention was paid to performance and reception and therefore to Stoppard the player. There is a very strong case for saying that all plays need to be studied in relation to performance and reception. This becomes an unanswerable one when performance and reception are themselves the explicit themes of a particular play. This is so with *Rosencrantz*, which is therefore an example of what I have called the 'theatre of theatre'. I, and a number of other critics, suggest the need for a critical practice which pays less attention to lists of possible influences and more to the way in which performance influences reception. We represent

Stoppard as somebody who is much more at home in the theatre than in a study. He may not have been a professional actor, like Harold Pinter was, and only directs plays on an occasional basis. Yet his instincts and intuitions are still essentially theatrical rather than academic ones. One of the most convincing arguments along these lines is, unfortunately, not widely available. Cheryl Faroane, an American Ph.D. student, interviewed those concerned with a number of Stoppard productions in both Britain and America. The picture of Stoppard which she builds up is of a committed, hard-working theatrical practitioner. It is rather a different one from that which tends to emerge from Stoppard's own mannered, rather narcissistic interviews.

Rosencrantz quickly became labelled as a difficult play, for critics if not for audiences, because of the intellectual context which was deemed essential for its appreciation. A lot of this difficulty was in the eye of the beholders. The play still presents problems, even when it is no longer taken as a location for a game of 'spot the allusion'. I suspect that many students will be puzzled by the fact that it is not 'about' anything in the conventional sense of the word. It is, at least initially, much easier to come to terms with a play which deals with naturalistic themes. John Osborne's *Look Back in Anger* (1956) is 'about' class and gender relationships. Its representation of them is a relatively transparent or mimetic one, so an essential part of studying it would be to consider it in the context of the 1950s. This might take the form of theatre history in which the main question would be whether Osborne's play was really articulating something 'about' these issues which other ones were not. A more rewarding approach would be to examine these representations, together with ones of nostalgia and imperialism, within the wider context of the culture and society of the 1950s. This might produce an interpretation which stressed that Osborne's text articulated, but did not always resolve, a number of this society's basic contradictions. These might include tensions between affluence and austerity, mobility and stability, present and past. The analysis would probably need to refer to historical events other than those which took place during the 1950s, such as Edwardian imperialism, the Spanish Civil War and the decline of the music-halls. Although such an essentially materialist argument is not without its own methodological difficulties, it should not leave students wondering what *Look Back in Anger* might be 'about'. Interpretations of the play might differ, even though there is a broad consensus over what information is required to interpret it.

Rosencrantz is 'about' the theatre and theatricality and is therefore not quite so easy to contextualize. The decision I had to make when thinking about how to approach the play was whether to spend as much time as possible proving this point about theatre and theatricality, or whether to shorten this essentially textual analysis in order to locate the play within the 1960s. My initial response was to opt for the latter approach mainly because it fitted in with my own critical practice. I was nevertheless still conscious of the fact that students, at universities as well as at schools and sixth-form colleges, often experience considerable difficulties with texts which are not obviously naturalistic or realistic ones. This point was emphasized to me at a sixth-form teachers' conference at which a number of the participants explained some of the problems which they and their students encountered when studying *Rosencrantz*. I therefore decided to set out in some detail the argument that the play is about the theatre and theatricality. My sequential reading might appear to be an inappropriate one for a play which is based around repetitions and cyclical patterns. I argue that it is essential to get a sense of the movement of the play in order to be able to come to terms with the vital questions about performance and reception. As will be apparent from my reservations about a particular style of Stoppard criticism, I do not let the textual analysis become a peg on which to hang up lists of literary and philosophical names. References to other writers, apart from Shakespeare, are used sparingly. Relationships between Stoppard and Beckett are dealt with separately in the Appendix. It is only really in the third part of the analysis that I try to locate *Rosencrantz* and some of Stoppard's other works within a wider cultural context. I suggest, for instance, that they need to be related to certain television and radio programmes as well as to various films. I am conscious, however, of only sketching in some of the relationships between such cultural forms and the society in which and for which they were produced.

I leave the discussion of *Rosencrantz* and the 1960s for class and seminar debate. If I was a part of this debate, I would be interested in responses to the proposition that it was a self-consciously theatrical decade. It placed a great emphasis on fashion, in common with other highly theatrical periods such as the Regency and Elizabethan ones. Clothes represented the costumes that were worn to play a rapid succession of parts. Fashion allowed people to fashion themselves. Everybody was sensitive about their 'image'; in other words, they were acutely aware of being watched while they played out their parts on the social stage. As the slang of the decade reminds us, these actors were forever worrying about whether they were in the right 'scene'. Stoppard himself was a dedicated follower of sixties' fashions and, even today, to some extent still looks and sounds like a King's Road dandy. He modelled himself on Mick Jagger, although was careful not to include the bad boy characteristics in his performance of this part. He was always the mildly sardonic one rather than the wild one. The sixties got a playwright in its own image when he became an overnight success as a result of the performance of *Rosencrantz* at the Edinburgh Fringe Festival in 1966. Overnight success, like the instant personalities which could be acquired through fashion, was the name of the social game. Everyone or everything had to be new. The fact that Stoppard had been establishing quite a promising reputation as a writer before 1966 was not allowed to get in the way of this rags to riches mythology. Ronald Bryden's review of the Fringe production in the *Observer* announced that a major playwright was having his work performed in relative obscurity. *Rosencrantz*, parts of which had been written on a Ford Foundation grant in Germany, was in fact only staged on the Fringe because the Royal Shakespeare Company had not taken up an option on it at the last moment. Stoppard was nevertheless cast as an obscure playwright who was going to hit the big time. He was plucked from the chorus line, or from his role as an attendant lord at the theatrical court, by a telegram from the National Theatre. A new playwright was needed for this new theatrical enterprise.

Rosencrantz became a smash hit on both sides of the Atlantic. Stoppard may have written his own theatrical script, with a bit of help from Shakespeare, but the equally theatrical cultural script for his instant success was written in accordance with sixties' mythologies. Heroes were, for instance, expected to be classless ones. Stoppard fitted this bill without too much difficulty. Although he had attended a very minor public school, he had gone straight into journalism rather than following a more conventional route to university. The fact that he was born and brought up in Czechoslovakia, and then had lived in Singapore and India, before coming to England as a small boy made him difficult to place in class terms. It also meant that he carried a set of potentially cosmopolitan associations, which gave British interviewers something different to discuss. Stoppard likes to represent himself as being a bit of a loner during the sixties. Everyone else, he claimed, was writing about 'Vietnam or housing'. The decade certainly produced more than its fair share of committed plays, although there is a sense in which the themes of Stoppard's script also chimed in very well with those of the social script. He was a new, young face who appeared to have little time for older faces like Shakespeare. The fact that he was pushing thirty when

Rosencrantz became an overnight success did not prevent him from being offered up as a representative of the younger generation. His talent may have been to amuse rather than abuse but the irreverent, and seemingly iconoclastic, tone of his script gave the appearance of cultural protest. As implied, appearances were the only realities during the sixties. I spend a lot of time later on dealing in more precise terms with the essentially contradictory tone of *Rosencrantz* and some of the other earlier works. For the moment, I would like to suggest that Stoppard represented a kind of cheeky chic which was as much a part of the sixties' scene as plays about Vietnam. There is obviously more to be said about what might be described as the moment of *Rosencrantz*. All that I have had time to do here is sketch in an argument which emphasizes that it was no cultural accident that a play about theatricality, written by a relatively young dandy, became such a success. As Ronald Hayman puts it, Stoppard appeared 'at the right moment'.

This analysis does not locate *Rosencrantz* within the sixties as firmly as it might do and it also does not offer an extended biography of Stoppard himself. I refer in passing to biographical details when they seem relevant to a more purely textual point. For example, I suggest that Stoppard's 'émigré' status helps to explain his related obsessions with childhood and Englishness. Other critics might have developed such a point into a more detailed psychological reading of the texts. I was wary of doing this because I do not possess the relevant skills. Although such an approach ought to be another item on the agenda for class or seminar room discussion, I would advise a certain amount of caution. One of the major themes that I develop in the third part of my argument is that writers in general, and Stoppard in particular, are liars. I am therefore rather suspicious of the kind of criticism which abstracts details from the interviews that Stoppard has given and then seeks to locate them within the texts. I found these interviews more of a hindrance than a help and so, unlike most Stoppard critics, have used them very sparingly. I do not think that an interview with Shakespeare would offer instant solutions to the problems of interpreting *Hamlet* and it is dangerous to assume that Stoppard himself provides either the best, or more importantly the most truthful, account of himself and his works.

The danger in spending a lot of time studying a single text is that you can end up knowing it very well, but still not understanding it. I found myself in this position while working my way through the criticism on *Rosencrantz*. It was only when I began to branch out and study Stoppard's other works that I began to understand this particular play. It often takes what appear to be indirections to find directions out. This is my justification for dealing with some of these other works in the third part of the analysis. I only select four texts, so my aim is not to provide an overview of Stoppard's career. I do not, for example, consider his radio and television plays, film scripts, adaptations for the stage or indeed some of his more recent full-length stage plays. My concern is, rather, to illustrate how these four texts play variations on the themes of *Rosencrantz*. This provides an extension of the analysis of the set text rather than a complete break from it. The third part of the argument also tries to define critical terms such as parody, camp and postmodernism, which are essential to an understanding of *Rosencrantz*. A handful of critics suggest that Stoppard never fulfilled the promise of his first major play. My own view is that *Travesties* is his most distinctive, innovative, and therefore best play. I do not, however, want to force this particular point of view on anybody. My argument is that, if you understand *Travesties*, then you will be in a better position to appreciate what happens in *Rosencrantz*. The comparison between the two plays can work just at the level of explanation. The fact that it may involve broader, more evaluative judgements at least poses the question of whether *Rosencrantz* deserves its reputation as a 'contemporary classic'. It is a question which is not raised if the emphasis remains on the set text itself.

I mentioned that this part of the argument includes a consideration of parody, camp and postmodernism. Although the recent critical work on parody reveals that it is a more complicated term than it is often assumed to be, it is nevertheless one that is a common part of critical vocabulary. The same may not be true of camp and postmodernism. I refer to Stoppard as a camp writer in much the same way as I might refer to Jane Austen as a realist one. Labels are often difficult to attach to any writer, but camp is the one which I think fits Stoppard the best. I base my interpretation on an essay which Susan Sontag published on the subject in the same year that *Rosencrantz* was a hit at the Edinburgh Festival. The term is often used in a jokey, frivolous way and there is nothing wrong in this, particularly as camp is about frivolity. Sontag writes that

the whole point of Camp is to dethrone the serious. Camp is playful, anti-serious. More precisely, Camp involves a new, more complex relation to 'the serious'. One can be serious about the frivolous, and frivolous about the serious.

As far as I am concerned, this offers the best explanation of what takes place in *Rosencrantz* and in some of Stoppard's later works. Any one who proposes to take camp itself seriously is in danger of getting painfully trapped within the paradoxes that Sontag outlines. I shall, nevertheless, be using the term as part of my critical vocabulary. As will become apparent, camp offers a solution to the problems of being a dandy in modern society. Stoppard critics often use dandyism as a term of abuse. I propose to consider Stoppard's dandyism in much the same way as I would deal with Jane Austen's realism: as an artistic position which requires explanation rather than as something which can just be dismissed out of hand. Harold Hobson suggested back in 1966 that *Rosencrantz* could be compared with the writings of Alain Robbe-Grillet and therefore with the *nouveau roman*. This context has, rather surprisingly, rarely been fully explored. Some of the more recent Stoppard critics, such as Tim Brassell, are nevertheless posing important questions about whether Stoppard ought to be considered as a postmodernist writer. My brief survey of postmodernism also tends to pose the question rather than provide anything but a tentative answer. Postmodernism is a complex subject and my survey does not do justice to it. I include it, however, as I think that it is important to give at least a sense of how Stoppard's work may be related to writings which are generally held to be more innovative than his own.

I ought just to say a brief word about reception in relation to my analysis of *Rosencrantz*. I have assumed, or implied, the kind of audience with which Stoppard is playing his theatrical games. I base this assumption on some remarks made by John Russell Taylor in his review of the original National Theatre production for *Plays and Players*. He was surprised that spectators were enjoying themselves so much, when what they were being offered was what he considered to be a pale imitation of well-known dramatic representations. He was forced to admit to the existence of at least two audiences: one consisting of connoisseurs of the avant-garde like himself, while the other was composed of more occasional theatre-goers. He saw the audience as being divided between professionals and amateurs. Although Stoppard addressed both these audiences in *Rosencrantz*, my assumption is that the play is aimed more at the amateur and the naturalistic expectations which they bring with them to the theatre. This fits in with the overall interpretation of Stoppard as a popular theatrical practitioner rather than a bookish, or academic, playwright.

Part One. The Theatre of Theatre in
Rosencrantz and Guildenstern are Dead

1. Ambushes on the Road to Elsinore

Ambushing the audience (pp. 9–13)

Funny things happen on the way to the theatre. They are part of the occasion. Even funnier things happen in the theatre itself if an audience's sense of occasion is undermined. There may be a breathless hush as the house lights go down. The stage lights merely reveal a bare set '*without any visible character*' (p. 9). Two unnamed characters pass the time by playing a repetitive game of heads or tails. This is not a spectator sport. Like the audience, they appear to be waiting for something to happen. Unlike the audience, they seem unconcerned that there is nothing to be done. They are also not worried by the fact that a relatively large sum of money is changing hands. The audience is much more concerned than they are about both the value of money and theatrical value for money.

The game, if it can be dignified as such, has been in progress for some time as one of the characters already has a lot of money in his purse. There are no clues as to why, when and how it started. The spectators are therefore placed in the position of late arrivals, who have to try to reconstruct what has, or perhaps has not, already happened. This is not playing fair with all those who arrived in good time, despite that hilarious incident on the way with the Buddhist monk and the lion-tamer. It would have made a much more entertaining play than this one. Are the two characters on stage Rosencrantz and Guildenstern – hardly the catchiest of names – or just attendants to these attendant lords? Dialogue is meant to supply such essential information, along with helpful little character notes. There are, however, no lines along the lines of 'to lose one coin, Mr Guildenstern, may be regarded as a misfortune; to lose seventy looks like carelessness'. There is not in fact any dialogue to speak of. Why do the coins always come down heads? Do I need my head examining for shelling out my own coins to wait around watching two actors waiting around? One of them at last delivers a whole sentence: 'There is an art to the building up of suspense' (p. 9). It is an art which Stoppard does not appear to know from his elbow. Or does he? He knows you know there is no conventional theatrical suspense. He even takes the words out of your mouth a little later on when one of the characters announces that the game is 'a bit of a bore' (p. 10). Perhaps the crafty fellow (let that be his character note) is playing a game with the audience. The spectators are the spectacle.

What do actors see when they look at an audience? A row of heads. Why are they interested in counting heads? Because they signify a full house and therefore a full purse. Ros and Guil get an improbable run, or row, of heads. They are, at one and the same time, playing a game of heads or tails and making a quick head count of the audience. Heads or tails itself may not be a recognized spectator sport, but this only encourages Stoppard to have some sport with the spectators. He denies them a conventional piece of scene setting. He reverses traditional distinctions between actors and spectators by making the actors watch the spectators.

Stoppard explained his theatrical practice in 1974 to the editors of *Theatre Quarterly*:

What was actually calculated was to entertain a roomful of people with the situation of Rosencrantz and Guildenstern at Elsinore. The chief thing that added one line to another line was that the combin-of the two should retain an audience's interest in some way. I tend to write through a series of small, large and microscopic ambushes – which might consist of a body falling out of a cupboard, or simply an unexpected word in a sentence.

The opening of *Rosencrantz* is one of these large ambushes. The emphasis on pure entertainment differentiates Stoppard from Bertolt Brecht, whose various strategies for either alienating or distancing audiences were closely related to explicitly ideological considerations. Stoppard runs the risk of alienating the audience at the beginning of *Rosencrantz* but only in order to entertain it. He wants to disinterest it only to interest it again in its own disinterestedness. He indulges in theatrical brinkmanship in order to be able to reveal his theatrical showmanship. His ambushes therefore lack the aggressive edge that is to be found in plays such as Peter Handke's *Offending the Audience* (1966). Jim Hunter gets it just right when he suggests that Stoppard is in the business of teasing audiences. The terminology that Stoppard himself uses to describe his theatrical practice, for instance ambush, emphasizes the point that his plays attempt to recover some of the pleasures of childhood games. He once claimed that he would rather have written the Winnie-the-Pooh stories than the complete works of Brecht.

The interview with *Theatre Quarterly* offers a useful introduction to the nature of Stoppard's dialogue in the earlier plays:

What there is, is a series of conflicting statements made by conflicting characters, and they tend to play a sort of infinite leap-frog. You know, an argument, a refutation, then a rebuttal of the refutation, then a counter-rebuttal, so that there is never any point in this intellectual leap-frog at which I feel *that* is the speech to stop it on, *that* is the last word.

The fact that, ironically enough, Stoppard is unable to stop, ambushes spectators with naturalistic assumptions and expectations about the theatre. These might include the belief that a well-made play should resolve rather than perpetuate conflict and contradiction. Behind this belief lies an assumption that characters ought to develop, and be seen to develop, a consistent point of view. The game of 'infinite leap-frog', which provides another example of how Stoppard associates his plays with childhood games, teases spectators who expect both linear narratives and consistent characters. Guil lists the 'possible explanations' (p. 12) for the run of heads, which include ones based on accident as well as design, but is unable to adjudicate between them. It is therefore difficult for the spectators to construct their own character notes for him. The spectators have to start off playing the 'which is which' game. When they have worked out differences between Ros and Guil, they then graduate to the 'who represents what' game. Even though it is impossible to say whether Guil represents accident or design, some sort of list can still be compiled. Ros is practical, prosaic and rather stupid, whereas Guil is more emotional, poetic and intelligent. Stoppard suggests, in terms which once again emphasize the links with childhood, that Guil acts as a *'nursemaid'* (p. 29) to Ros. Yet Ros and Guil's characters are shown to be fluid and interchangeable rather than fixed and permanent. They are, at best, different sides of the same coin. Stoppard ambushes the spectators and their character notes in Act Two by flipping this coin over and letting Ros play nursemaid to Guil. The old tease changes the rules in the middle of the game.

Not a mouse stirring (pp. 9–17)

There is more teasing to be teased out of the opening of *Rosencrantz*. Renaissance plays often begin with minor characters such as servants, soldiers, attendant lords and the citizen in the street, who hurriedly set the scene and then hurriedly disappear from it. *Hamlet* itself opens with just such a moment. Barnardo enters to relieve Francisco of sentry duty on the ramparts at Elsinore:

BARNARDO: Who's there?

FRANCISCO: Nay, answer me. Stand and unfold yourself.
BARNARDO: Long live the King!
FRANCISCO: Barnardo?
BARNARDO: He.
FRANCISCO: You come most carefully upon your hour.
BARNARDO: 'Tis now struck twelve. Get thee to bed, Francisco. (I.1.1–7)

Unlike Ros and Guil, these two soldiers call each other by their names almost immediately. Other information is also rapidly conveyed: there is a king and the time is midnight. This short exchange evokes mood and atmosphere very effectively. Francisco's 'Nay, answer me. Stand and unfold yourself' suggests the suspicion and deception that characterize the Danish court. Barnardo has in fact muddled up the military drill: it is Francisco's job to say 'Who's there?'. This basic slip suggests anxiety and also prepares the way for the whole series of broken ceremonies or 'maimèd rites' (V.1.215) that is to come. The fact that both men are sentries, or members of the Watch, points forward to the way in which the other characters watch, or spy on, each other. They have one more function to fulfil before Francisco at least can get back to the dressing-room for a slow game of heads or tails, or whatever else might pass the time. They have to introduce, by name, new characters:

BARNARDO: If you do meet Horatio and Marcellus,
    The rivals of my watch, bid them make haste.
FRANCISCO: I think I hear them. Stand ho! Who is there? (I.1.12–14)

These two minor characters quickly and effectively get the action under way, while at the same time establishing the mood of the play.

Francisco's watch has apparently been quiet and uneventful: 'Not a mouse stirring' (I.1.10). This idiomatic phrase annoyed Voltaire, who claimed that it was out of place in a great tragedy. The event is only referred to, however, for the quick contrast it offers to the extraordinary event which is about to take place with the entrance of the Ghost. Shakespeare does not actually show his audience Francisco watching and waiting on the ramparts for a mouse to stir. This is not the stuff of Renaissance tragedy. Something broadly equivalent to it is nevertheless the stuff of Stoppard's comedy. Ros and Guil do not just set the scene, they are it. They do not convey information, suggest atmosphere and then make way for more important events. On the contrary, they do not seem able to depart. It is as if Barnardo and Francisco had suddenly developed an intense if somewhat absurd interest in the nocturnal habits of the Danish mouse, which they pass the time by discussing.

Ros and Guil are forced to improvise their subjects for conversation because they have no information to impart to the expectant audience. They may discuss monkeys being thrown up into the air rather than Danish mice, but the effect is the same. They also do so in the kind of colloquial language to which Voltaire objected. Stoppard is spinning a coin with an actor on one side and a spectator on the other. Actors are supposed to tell spectators what is happening or about to happen, but these two would welcome such information as well. The chances must be that the spectators are better informed about what happens in *Hamlet* than these particular actors in it are. Terence Hawkes puts it well when he says that in western cultures any production of *Hamlet* has 'always already begun' before the spectators get to the theatre. Nobody, apart from Ros and Guil, comes fresh to the play. This does not mean that everybody in the audience will have read or seen *Hamlet* before, but rather that they will have been exposed to the popular mythology which surrounds the play. Tony Hancock auditions for the part of Hamlet after he has been written out of a radio soap opera in *The Bowmans* (BBC TV, 1961). He delivers the opening of the 'To be, or not to be' soliloquy, but does so in the exaggerated rural accent that he has developed for the part of Joshua Merryweather. This scene reinforces the popular mythology that Hamlet is the one part that every actor wants to play, while at the same time deflating the part's importance through the clash between Shakespearian English and broad mummersetshire. Hancock never gets to play the lad himself and has to make television advertisements instead. Advertisements encode popular mythologies. One for Carling Black Label shows Hamlet, dressed in black, conversing with Yorick's skull. He drops it, but manages to trap and control it using a mixture of football and basketball techniques. Another character, presumably Horatio, makes a very stagey entrance dressed in Elizabethan costume. He addresses Hamlet in Shakespeare-speak: 'My noble Lord Hamlet'. He then abruptly changes the idiom to football-speak: 'Over here, son. On me head'. He gets the skull and then passes it back to Hamlet, who sends it into the audience with a stylish overhead kick. It lands in one of the theatre boxes where Jack the Lad is watching the performance as well as drinking a pint of Black Label. The skull delivers the slogan 'I bet he drinks Carling Black Label' after Hamlet and Horatio have performed an imitation of football players celebrating a goal. A familiar image of Hamlet is being reinforced. He dresses in black, which corresponds to his moody nature, and he is either mad or morbid because he talks to skulls. Most Shakespearian critics believe that Hamlet ought in fact to be wearing clothes which he has borrowed from the pirates for this graveyard scene. Yet he only becomes instantly recognizable through his black clothes, which is presumably one of the reasons why he is being used to advertise a black label lager. Similarly, Ophelia is always signified by white clothes. Identification is aided by the sign language which is conveyed by props such as Yorick's skull or Ophelia's Pre-Raphaelite garland of flowers. The message of this particular commercial appears to be that even Hamlet would become the life and soul of the party after he has had a drink of Black Label. His tragedy is simply that it was not available in his time as the instant cure for all his troubles. This commercial acts out in miniature what happens in *Rosencrantz*: it draws attention to its theatricality and juxtaposes Shakespearian English with modern colloquialisms. It affirms the importance of *Hamlet* by appropriating its cultural sign language, while at the same time denying this importance through the juxtaposition of the Shakespearian and the contemporary. Hawkes's point is that a performance of *Hamlet* has 'always already begun' for spectators who have been exposed to the popular mythology that surrounds, and indeed engulfs, the play. Stoppard turns this to comic advantage by allowing his actors to remain more ignorant than his spectators.

Guil is the more perplexed of the two about the improbable run of heads. This is not because he is the loser, as money is just a toy in this world of childhood games and pranks. He is concerned instead with the meaning of this event. He has to be because there is nothing else to talk about, let alone write home about. Almost everything prior to this particular moment has no meaning or existence. Like a child, Guil has an absorbing sense of the present, but only a hazy recollection of the past and a dim conception of a future. Stoppard underlines this point, both in the play itself and in his subsequent comments on it, by stressing that Ros and Guil need to be seen as innocent children. This representation effectively ambushes spectators who are trying to compile character notes by piecing together information about pre-play events and relationships. Guil may be a child, but he expresses his perplexity in pompous and seemingly erudite terms. Stoppard passes the time by playing with a coin that has a child on one side and a philosophy professor on the other:

If we postulate, and we just have, that within un-, sub- or supernatural forces *the probability* is that the law of probability will not operate as a factor, then we must accept that the probability of the *first* part will not operate as a factor, in which case the law of probability *will* operate as a factor within un-, sub- or supernatural forces. And since it obviously hasn't been doing so, we can take it that we are not held within un-, sub- or supernatural forces after all; in all probability, that is.

(p. 14)

Guil is speaking in two languages here which eventually clash with each other. The idiomatic reference to probability, 'in all probability, that is', undermines the tortuous philosophical use of the word earlier on. Just as the lager commercial clashes a formal language with a more informal one, so Stoppard juxtaposes the philosophical with the colloquial.

What is happening on stage when Guil delivers this filibuster against silence and fear? Ros, the on-stage audience, pays no attention whatsoever to it. Guil's rhetorical attempts to interest his audience fall on very stony ground. Ros is either cutting his fingernails or thinking about doing so. He acts out the theatre audience's feelings of boredom. The actor–spectator coin is being flipped over again: Ros is an actor who nevertheless plays the part of a spectator. The fact that, here and elsewhere, an on-stage audience is shown to be inattentive makes the theatre audience very self-conscious about its role. Guil begins his filibuster on the unpromising theme of 'The scientific approach to the examination of phenomena' (p. 13). He ends it, however, with a series of more personal statements. Ros pays no attention to this leap-frogging from the objective to the subjective. He responds, sounding remarkably like Peter Cook, with his own variation on the theme of scientific approaches:

Another curious scientific phenomenon is the fact that the fingernails grow after death, as does the beard. (p. 14)

His concentration has wandered off. He returns to Guil's original proposition, unaware of how the argument has developed. His own theme is also useless information, or at least information which is only useful in that it passes the time. This would have passed anyway, but perhaps not so quickly. Stoppard teases the theatre audience by following the repetitious game of heads or tails with very average monologues on the laws of averages and probability. He makes it self-conscious about its boredom by showing it a reflection of itself on stage.

The fact that Ros and Guil do not listen to each other also produces comic misunderstandings. They drift into a cross-talk act over the proposition that if six monkeys were tossed up into the air they would come down as often on their heads as their tails:

GUIL: ... if six monkeys were ...
ROS: Game?
GUIL: Were they?
ROS: Are you?   (p. 10)

The law of averages is a bit of a bore. The idea of six game, or promiscuous, monkeys being thrown up into the air suggests a more intriguing subject, particularly if there is some time to pass. It is very quiet, not a mouse stirring. You suddenly look out of the window and see a man in a white coat and pyjamas, whose face is covered with shaving foam. He starts lobbing randy monkeys up into the air. We can probably postulate that, in all probability, he is an eccentric scientist. It passes the time to consider other explanations. He may be a certified lunatic, a circus performer, an actor rehearsing for a part in a Stoppard play, Stoppard himself ...

Another curious comic phenomenon in this play is that old jokes never die. Ros and Guil have no past, and as they eventually discover, no future. It is extraordinary the tricks that memory plays. Ros and Guil can barely remember the last thing that was said to them, let alone anything about their backgrounds. This allows Stoppard to remember a few jokes about amnesia, or rather the same one a few times which may be just as difficult. Such jokes are similar to graffiti ones. *Hamlet* has been described as a gothic cathedral of a play. Stoppard is a graffiti artist who chalks up his witty one-liners on its sacred walls. Besides the one about amnesia, he does a good line in jokes about death: 'Death followed by eternity ... the worst of both worlds' (p. 53). Once again, a colloquial, popular form of language is contrasted with a more formal one.

Ros and Guil, after a number of false starts, eventually manage to remember why they are on the road to Elsinore. They embellish upon their fragmentary recollections like actors doing an improvisation. They desperately seek to give their summons, and therefore themselves, heroic credentials. Their rhetorical flights of fancy are brought down to earth by idiomatic language. The tone is therefore mock-heroic. 'Stand, ho! Who is there?' does not have quite the same ring to it when it is rendered in modern, colloquial English:

ROS: That's it – pale sky before dawn, a man standing on his saddle to bang on
        the shutters – shouts – What's all the row about?! Clear off! – But then he
        called our names. You remember that – this man woke us up.   (p. 15)

The rhetoric is also undermined by the fact that, despite the 'extreme urgency' (p. 15) of the summons, Ros and Guil are just passing the time in their attempts to recall it. The message, as Ros self-importantly remembers, is that speed was of the essence. He describes it, as a spectator might do, but is unable to act upon it. Ros and Guil are being summoned to play their parts in *Hamlet*. These are minor ones so the messenger does not waste time on directions. He calls out the names of the parts, but is not specific about which of the two actors is to play which one. The theatre audience has to grope towards identifications of both Ros and Guil. This is not made easy as the old tease suggests that the attendant lords themselves are unclear about their own identities. There is no 'last word' to this improvisation about the messenger. It merely grinds to a halt, much as Ros and Guil have done, and has to be replaced by another game.

The sound of a band offers welcome relief, as do other forms of play, to the sounds of silence. Ros is at first unable to believe his ears and then is cheered up by the thought of a further diversion. The sound of distant drums comes as a welcome relief to the theatre audience as well. There may at last be some sustained action. Guil chooses this moment to expound another of his philosophical treatises, this time on the relativity and unreliability of sensory perceptions. It is necessary to establish this dramatic context since Guil's speech on the sighting of unicorns is sometimes used to suggest that he is a philosophical character in a play of ideas. Ros, the on-stage audience, once again pays no attention to his friend's philosophizing. When it has finished, he continues to talk about the band. Such a disinterested reaction from the on-stage audience mirrors the response of the theatre audience. Guil is disappointed that it is a band rather than a unicorn which breaks the monotony. He wants to associate himself with unicorns and therefore with mystery, mythology and poetry. The opening moments of the play suggest that both he and Ros ought to be associated with more prosaic creatures such as dormant mice.

Performance and patronage (pp. 17–26)

Rosencrantz draws attention to its theatricality by making the theatre audience self-conscious about its role. Theatricality is heightened with the arrival of the Player and the Tragedians, whose band it turns out to have been. Ros and Guil are given some direction at last. They may have thought that they were actors, but the Player immediately identifies them as spectators. He therefore tries to interest them in a performance. He gives them one for free while he peddles his theatrical wares. He becomes a seedy salesman who can do them a nice little number, as well as a music-hall comedian who has seen it all before. He is able to play a gushing theatrical impresario who can transport his customers 'into a world of intrigue and illusion' (p. 18) and a shady night-club owner who nudges, winks and says no more. He also plays himself. Ros and Guil are baffled at being taken for spectators, but the Player suggests that actors and spectators, performers and patrons are merely interchangeable parts:

PLAYER: ... I recognized you at once –
ROS: And who are we?
PLAYER: – as fellow artists.
ROS: I thought we were gentlemen.
PLAYER: For some of us it is performance, for others, patronage. They are two sides of the same coin, or, let us say, being as there are so many of us, the same side of two coins. (*Bows again.*) Don't clap too loudly – it's a very old world. (p. 18)

The final remark, which echoes Archie Rice in Osborne's *The Entertainer* (1957), is designed to make the spectators, both on and off the stage, feel self-conscious about their roles.

The Player's repertoire of plays provides a marked contrast to what *Rosencrantz* itself has to offer. Stoppard has found another way of teasing the theatre audience. Perhaps its members would really feel more at home patronizing one of the Player's performances:

... Deaths and disclosures, universal and particular, dénouements both unexpected and inexorable, transvestite melodrama on all levels including the suggestive ... we can do you rapiers or rape or both, by all means, faithless wives and ravished virgins – flagrante delicto at a price, but that comes under realism for which there are special terms. Getting warm, am I? (p. 18)

Ros, the innocent abroad, does not quite understand what is being offered by this king of leers. Unlike the theatre audience, he is unable to see the sex and violence that the Player is dangling in front of him. As actors and spectators are just different sides of the same coin, the Player hopes to get a response from him by suggesting that he might like to participate in one of these shows himself. The theatre audience is being teased by not being offered the same option. Theatrical value for money, which was dealt with rather obliquely at the beginning of *Rosencrantz*, is now presented more explicitly as the link between patronage and performance:

ROS: And how much?
PLAYER: To take part?
ROS: To watch.
PLAYER: Watch what?
ROS: A private performance.
PLAYER: How private?
ROS: Well, there are only two of us. Is that enough?
PLAYER: For an audience, disappointing. For voyeurs, about average.

(p. 19)

Ros and Guil are being cast as voyeurs in relation to this particular performance but, as will become more apparent later on, they are also voyeurs in their relationship with the theatre audience. Ros and the Player continue to haggle over money, although Ros's innocence about what is being offered continues to be the real stumbling block. The Player practically spells it out when he says that 'we'll stoop to anything if that's your bent' (p. 19), but Ros probably just thinks that he suffers from backache.

Guil is a spectator while Ros and the Player act out their parts in this scene about patrons and performers. Ros makes all the running, which includes an attempt to introduce himself and his friend Guil to the Tragedians. As indicated, the problem is that the messenger forgot to tell them who was supposed to be whom. They would probably have forgotten anyway. Guil broods about the meaning of the unexpected arrival of the Tragedians, who appear to have ambushed the attendant lords on the road to Elsinore. The chance mention of chance stirs him into engaging the Player in a debate about accident and design. The Player shows that he too is an accomplished leap-frogger when he argues the case for both:

We have no control. Tonight we play to the court. Or the night after. Or to the tavern. Or not. (p. 20)

His facetious tone goads Guil into trying to put on a dignified show:

GUIL: Perhaps I can use my influence.
PLAYER: At the tavern?
GUIL: At the court. I would say I have some influence.
PLAYER: Would you say so?
GUIL: I have influence yet.

23

PLAYER: Yet what?

  (GUIL *seizes the* PLAYER *violently*.)

GUIL: I have influence!   (p. 20)

Guil drops into Elizabethan English in an attempt to impress the Player. His ironic claim to 'have influence yet' may be compared in terms of construction to Brutus's 'O Julius Caesar, thou art mighty yet' (V.3.94) and the Duchess of Malfi's 'I am Duchess of Malfi still' (IV.2.139). The Player makes fun of this striving after rich cadence and high sentence. Guil's quest for importance, like his quest for a quest, is doomed to disappointment.

Guil becomes even more violent moments later when the Player volunteers to stage 'a private and uncut performance of the Rape of the Sabine Women'. Guil, the spectator, is offered the opportunity to act 'either part' (p. 20). Ironically, his objections to the theatre of violence take a violent form. He feels that such a production would be beneath a man of his influence:

It could have been – it didn't have to be *obscene* . . . It could have been – a bird out of season, dropping bright-feathered on my shoulder . . . It could have been a tongueless dwarf standing by the road to point the way . . . I was *prepared*. But it's this, is it? No enigma, no dignity, nothing classical, portentous, only this – a comic pornographer and a rabble of prostitutes . . .   (p. 21)

The stage directions indicate that he is '*shaking with rage and fright*' when delivering this speech: rage at the Player and fright at the possibility that there might be nothing beyond an impurely physical existence. His quest for meaning and significance once again rebounds comically on him. The combination of 'bird' and 'dropping' is an unfortunate one. The image of the 'tongueless dwarf' on the verge of the road verges on the grotesque. He also unwittingly provides a review of *Rosencrantz* itself when he lists what is wrong with the Player's repertoire: 'No enigma, no dignity, nothing classical, portentous.' The fact that, here and elsewhere, *Rosencrantz* reviews itself heightens its theatricality. It holds a mirror up to itself. Guil may want to object to the morality of staging a representation of the Rape of the Sabine Women, but he does not help his case by dismissing it as being unclassical. It took place, after all, in Roman times.

Ros eventually tumbles to what the Tragedians have to offer. Stoppard parodies the responses of heterosexual males to pornography by making him move from embarrassed interest to heated outrage. Perhaps these responses are just different sides of the same coin. Ros takes a purely academic interest in the subject:

Well, I'm not really the type of man who – no, but don't hurry off – sit down and tell us about some of the things people ask you to do – (p. 22)

The Player will have nothing to do with this fumbling approach or the single coin which is supposed to pay for the peep-show, so Ros works himself up into a state of moral indignation:

Filth! Disgusting – I'll report you to the authorities – *perverts*! I know your game all right, it's all filth! (p. 22)

The irony is that this is one of the few games that he does not know.

Stoppard plays the comic pornographer with the theatre audience. He appears to be promising new directions in the form of this peep-show, but then only offers another game of heads or tails. Ros and Guil invariably opt for what they know when faced with the prospect of change. They literally and metaphorically want to play it safe. The Player has been running rings around them, but the game of heads or tails allows them to regain a certain amount of control. They win Alfred, or at least a performance from Alfred, which amounts to the same thing. Guil leads the frightened boy actor down to the footlights:

(GUIL *looks around, at the audience.*)
GUIL: You and I, Alfred – we could create a dramatic precedent here. (*And* ALFRED, *who has been near to tears, starts to sniffle.*) Come, come, Alfred, this is no way to fill the theatres of Europe. (p. 24)

Alfred, who always plays victims, is himself the victim of the Player's theatrical hype. He is represented as the main attraction in the various shows that are outlined, yet the reality is very different. Stoppard uses him to illustrate the artificiality of the theatre. This is not done just by revealing that the woman's part is played by a little boy. The inevitable gap between theatrical promise and performance is made apparent, at a more general level, by showing Alfred struggling in and out of his costumes while the Player provides an inappropriate running commentary. Guil, addressing the theatre audience as well as Alfred, reviews the Player's repertoire when he says that 'this is no way to fill the theatres of Europe'. He also reviews Stoppard's play. Can it hope to 'fill the theatres of Europe' when it offers repetition rather than development?

Ros and Guil do not develop or change their attitudes towards the theatre. They merely reiterate their fixed positions: Guil wants something classical, while Ros, despite his better feelings, is interested in the more popular end of the market. Stoppard suggests that these two positions are only different sides of the same coin:

GUIL: ... Well then – one of the Greeks, perhaps? You're familiar with the great tragedies of antiquity, are you? The great homicidal classics? Matri, patri, fratri, sorori, uxori and it goes without saying –

ROS: Saucy –

GUIL: – Suicidal – hm? Maidens aspiring to godheads –

ROS: And vice versa –

GUIL: Your kind of thing, is it?

PLAYER: Well, no, I can't say it is, really. We're more of the blood, love and rhetoric school. (p. 25)

Guil undermines his own case for the cultural superiority of classical drama. Ros's overlapping commentary reinforces the point.

Stoppard likes to make his audiences wait. The Tragedians are ready to stage their play within the play. Ros and Guil have, as might be expected, conventional ideas about theatrical staging as well as subject matter. They want the Player to make a suitably dramatic entrance, which is ironically something which they themselves have failed to do. He explains that he is always on stage dressed for the part. This exchange continues the examination of theatricality, while at the same time holding up the possibility of some sustained theatrical action. *Rosencrantz* holds a mirror up to itself and to theatre in general. It offers a sustained exploration of relationships between performers and patrons rather than sustained action.

Peep-shows (pp. 26–9)

The Player is persuaded to exit to make an entrance. Ros bends down to pick up a coin, which is obviously a dangerous thing to do given the Player's line in sexual innuendo. This coin has landed on tails. This suggests that there will be a dramatic change. *Rosencrantz* is about to be flipped over to *Hamlet*. Such a conclusion is less clear-cut when watching the play in performance. Indeed, uncertainty about what might happen next allows Stoppard to stage another of his large ambushes. Ros and Guil attempt to make a speedy exit before the Player's entrance. The theatre audience is teased by being shown spectators who try to walk out but who are forced to remain where they are. Ros and Guil are ambushed by a dumb show or piece of mime. It is based around events from *Hamlet*, although this should not be immediately apparent. The stage directions in the first edition underlined this point by drawing attention to a superficial resemblance between Hamlet and the Player. There should also be a resemblance between the mime that Hamlet and Ophelia perform and some of the plays in the Player's repertoire. Hamlet bursts into Ophelia's closet in a very dishevelled state. Is he passionately in love with Ophelia or has he been mentally disturbed by the appearance of the Ghost? Polonius believes that Hamlet's actions are those of somebody who is mad for love:

> This is the very ecstasy of love,
> Whose violent property fordoes itself
> And leads the will to desperate undertakings
> As oft as any passion under heaven
> That does afflict our natures.

(II.1.102–6)

He implies that, with Hamlet in this desperate state, Ophelia can count herself lucky not to have been raped. It should not be clear to Stoppard's audience during the early stages of this mime whether it is watching a pornographic peep-show or an adaptation from Shakespeare. Can spectators really tell the difference between the two? Perhaps they are just different sides of the same coin. Stoppard tests the audience's theatrical palate, in much the same way as advertisers lay on tests to see who can really tell the difference between margarine and butter. This is the first part of the ambush. The second part of it relates to the way in which the audience's first impressions of *Hamlet* in its new context are of a play without words. Harry Levin puts it well when he suggests that audiences traditionally respond to the play like opera fans: they wait for the famous speeches and soliloquies as if they were arias. Stoppard denies his audience this pleasure.

The stage directions in *Hamlet* indicate that Rosencrantz and Guildenstern make their first appearance as part of a procession led by Claudius and Gertrude. In Stoppard's play, Ros and Guil are already on stage so they are ambushed by this procession. They are inexperienced actors who are in the wrong place, much to the annoyance of the other members of the cast. Stoppard's stage directions indicate that these two coarse actors threaten to disrupt the whole performance: 'ROS *and* GUIL *still adjusting their clothing for* CLAUDIUS's *presence*' (p. 27). Although their

27

parts are written out for this scene without stumbles and pauses, these need to be inserted. Stumbling is the operative word for what is happening here. First of all, Ros and Guil stumble into the performance of *Hamlet* without a clue about what is going on. Claudius assumes that they already know something about 'Hamlet's transformation' (p. 27), but it is all news to them. Shakespeare's Rosencrantz and Guildenstern are accused by Hamlet of being bad actors whose looks betray their purposes. They are, in other words, unable to disguise their feelings. Stoppard's Ros and Guil are also unable to put up a convincing front. They should therefore greet both the form and content of Claudius's welcoming speech with incredulous stares as well as hurried glances at each other. Secondly, both Claudius and Gertrude stumble in their attempts to differentiate between Hamlet's friends. This continues the theme of fluid, interchangeable identities. Thirdly, Ros and Guil stumble about in their attempts to play the courtier. They bow at the wrong moments and their stage business with their hats ought to resemble slapstick. All this is in sharp contrast to the stiff, formal and distinctly mannered way in which the other actors are playing Shakespeare. Stoppard parodies techniques of acting and production which would have seemed old-fashioned to members of the audience who might have seen, or just heard about, Peter Hall's 1966 Royal Shakespeare Company production of *Hamlet* with David Warner in the title-role. This offended those who believed that Shakespearian lines were there to be delivered in a stagey manner rather than just spoken. It contained, incidentally, a reasonably sympathetic representation of Rosencrantz and Guildenstern. The old-fashioned actors who make up Stoppard's Shakespearian cast treat Ros and Guil as coarse actors, although they themselves are in danger of being seen as such by spectators familiar with the RSC house-style in the 1960s. Such an audience reaction is likely to be even more marked today because of the virtual extinction of 'actor-manager' styles and techniques. Stoppard divides and rules his spectators: he teases the traditionalists by allowing his two comedians to steal the show, while at the same time pleasing the trendies with his parody of stuffy Shakespearian acting. He teases everyone by only allowing them to peep at *Hamlet*.

Language games (pp. 29–38)

The tantalizingly brief appearance of the Danish court sets up a clash between Shakespearian language and the looser, more idiomatic speech patterns that have so far dominated the play. It is a clash between the ancient and the modern, although it can also be seen as one between a public language, which does not necessarily have to be Shakespearian, and a more private one. Claudius represents the voice of an official discourse, whereas Ros and Guil opt for a more colloquial one. Their problem is that, after the Danish court has disappeared as mysteriously as it appeared, they are unable to make an easy transition from the public back to the more private discourse. Repetition makes them feel safe so it is hardly surprising that they rely so heavily upon clichés. A list of the ones that they use early on in the play might include the following: 'a bit of a bore' (p.10), 'a flicker of doubt' (p. 11), 'take some beating' (p. 12), 'it isn't your day' (p. 12), 'nothing to write home about' (p. 13), 'starting from scratch' (p. 16) and 'spreads it thinner' (p. 17). They panic when they find that they are unable to retreat to the safety of such familiar phrases:

ROS: I'm out of my step here –
GUIL: We'll soon be home and high – dry and home – I'll –
ROS: It's all over my *depth* –
GUIL: – I'll hie you home and –
ROS: – out of my head –
GUIL: – dry you high and –
ROS (*Cracking, high*):   – over my step over my head body! – I tell you it's all stopping to a death, it's boding to a depth, stepping to a head, it's all heading to a dead stop –
GUIL (*the nursemaid*):   There! . . . and we'll soon be home and dry . . . and *high* and dry . . .   (p. 29)

It is almost as if Ros and Guil have to learn the rudiments of speech again after they have been ambushed by the Danish court. There is, perhaps, a question for the theatre audience wrapped up in this representation of linguistic chaos. Do spectators experience a similar difficulty in adjusting to colloquial conversation after listening to Shakespeare's high sentences and mighty lines? If so, then Ros and Guil act out the parts of the spectators on the stage.

Clashes between Elizabethan language and modern colloquialisms are a basic ingredient in parodies of Shakespeare. *Beyond the Fringe* (1960) included a sketch called 'So That's the Way You Like It', which travesties Shakespeare's English history plays. Peter Cook and Jonathan Miller meet on the battlefield:

MILLER: Come, sir.
    Ah ha, a hit!
COOK: No sir, no hit, a miss! Come, sir, art foppish i' the mouth.

MILLER: Art more fop in the mouth than fop in steel.

             Oh, God, fair cousin, thou has done me wrong.

             Now is steel twixt gut and bladder interposed.

COOK: Oh, saucy Worcester, dost thou lie so still?

There is an allusion to a contemporary television programme in which a jury voted on whether newly released pop records would become 'hits' or 'misses'. The verbal comedy also depends on the gap between the Shakespearian and the modern meaning of 'saucy Worcester'.

Ros and Guil play a broadly similar game with Shakespearian language when they have managed to get their own clichés back in order. More specifically, they juxtapose some of Claudius's statements with their modern equivalents:

ROS: Well, he's changed, hasn't he? The exterior and inward man fails to resemble –

GUIL: Draw him on to pleasures – glean what afflicts him.

ROS: Something more than his father's death –

GUIL: He's always talking about us – there aren't two people living whom he dotes on more than us.

ROS: We cheer him up – find out what's the matter –

GUIL: Exactly, it's a matter of asking the right questions and giving away as little as we can. It's a game.   (p. 31)

Claudius's measured, well-rounded public speech gets chopped up into this kind of shorthand. It is, as indicated, partially translated into modern English. For instance, Claudius begins his speech to them, which is also addressed to the rest of the court, as follows:

> Something have you heard
> Of Hamlet's transformation, so call it,
> Sith nor th'exterior nor the inward man
> Resembles that it was.   (p. 27)

Ros translates the first part of this into colloquial English: 'Well, he's changed, hasn't he?' He leaves the second part of it more or less untouched, except that Guil does not give him the opportunity to finish it.

This exchange illustrates one of the familiar patterns to Ros and Guil's conversations. They start off in a bouncy, confident mood. Their concentration on the immediate past is a way of avoiding, or at least postponing, a discussion of the more perplexing questions about their existence. Yet they lose their impetus and momentum. Guil starts twisting his tongue around Renaissance and modern meanings of 'a king's remembrance' (p. 31) and Ros is in danger of getting lost. The quick-fire double-act gives way to a cross-talk one in which the participants are pulling in different directions. They are meant to be piecing together information about Hamlet, although he is eventually pushed to the side-lines. Ros and Guil end up discussing discussion instead:

ROS: What are you playing at?
GUIL: Words, words. They're all we have to go on. (*Pause.*) (p. 31)

They have taken this game of leap-frog about as far as it will go and therefore have to wait around for another game to suggest itself. The movement of their dialogues is therefore a circular one: silence followed by intense verbal activity which gradually peters out into silence again. The content of their dialogues is circular in the sense that they circle around the main issues such as how they are going to deal with Hamlet.

Stoppard has been teasing the audience throughout the play. Ros and Guil's circular conversations are just one of the many ambushes that he springs. Yet, except possibly when Guil leads Alfred down to the foot-lights, the dialogue between actors and spectators has been an indirect one. It becomes direct when Ros takes a long look at the theatre audience before announcing:

. . . I feel like a spectator – an appalling prospect. The only thing that makes it bearable is the irrational belief that somebody interesting will come on in a minute . . . (p. 31)

To pass the time, Guil follows him to the footlights: '. . . What a fine per-secution – to be kept intrigued without ever quite being enlightened' (p. 32). As actors they may be confronting the audience, although as spec-tators they are sympathizing with it. It is, conventionally, the writer's job to make sure that interesting people come on at regular intervals. Ronald Hayman suggests that Samuel Beckett gives the impression of having written *Waiting for Godot* (1955) 'without himself knowing how he was going to go on'. Stoppard gives a similar impression in *Rosencrantz*. It is, paradoxically, a highly contrived one which is designed to hold up a mirror to the writer. Just as the functions of and relationships between performers and patrons are debated, so the role of the writer is self-consciously drawn attention to by his apparent absence. Ros and Guil give the impression, albeit a misleading one, of being stranded on the stage and having to improvise their own script. Perhaps actors, spectators and writers are interchangeable parts.

Ros and Guil decide to pass the time by flipping verbal coins. The rules of this particular game are that questions have to be answered with questions. These rules become an end in themselves. Ros and Guil dramatize their own predicament as they only have questions about, but no answers to, the related questions of their existence and identity. The serves which put the conversational ball into play concentrate on questions about both the meaning of life and the meaning of names. Play, in this case wordplay, becomes a way of articulating as well as controlling anxieties. Ros and Guil may display their anxieties by not being able to provide answers, but they are nevertheless in control because they formulate the rules for the game. Ros is in fact very much at home so long as these rules provide a knowable, comforting framework. He reverts to his more obtuse self when Guil tries to leap-frog on to a new game involving Hamlet. There are a number of false starts before they are able to switch to a game in which Guil plays Hamlet and Ros plays himself. Their exchange provides another example of the way in which Stoppard reduces Shakespeare to shorthand:

ROS: Usurpation, then.
GUIL: He slipped in.
ROS: Which reminds me.
GUIL: Well, it would.
ROS: I don't want to be personal.
GUIL: It's common knowledge.
ROS: Your mother's marriage.
GUIL: He slipped in. (p. 37)

Shakespearian wordplay, based around Hamlet's belief that Claudius has slipped in between him and his chances of becoming king, is bounced off more idiomatic phrases such as 'I don't want to be personal'. Ros eventually has all the information at his disposal and attempts to summarize it:

To sum up: your father, whom you love, dies, you are his heir, you come back to find that hardly was the corpse cold before his young brother popped on to his throne and into his sheets, thereby offending both legal and natural practice. Now why exactly are you behaving in this extraordinary manner? (p. 38)

Ros ends with a question because, as in the verbal tennis game, he is unable to give answers. The facts that he has amassed are just useless information to him as he is unable to make connections between them. Clive Barker is probably right to suggest that Stoppard parodies the kind of questions asked in examinations by offering these summaries or 'story so far' routines. The reductive summary of literary texts is a familiar enough comic device, for instance *Monty Python*'s competition to summarize Proust. Ironically, Stoppard's own texts are now in danger of getting the 'story so far' treatment. The biter may therefore find himself bitten, although he is quite capable of biting back. Summaries of *Rosencrantz* which merely ask questions about the story will be as comically wide of the mark as Ros's attempts to put *Hamlet* in a nutshell. The answers will only come when it is realized that the play is about play and plays. Stoppard's theatre is the theatre of theatre.

A sense of not ending (pp. 38–9)

Ros and Guil, together with the theatre audience, are rescued from this language game about Hamlet, which is reaching a dead end, by the sudden reappearance of the man himself. Hamlet enters backwards, mocking the way in which Polonius walks. He and Polonius appear to be in the middle of an argument, although it is not particularly audible to the theatre audience. Shakespeare's text is made to seem incomprehensible, here and elsewhere, both because it is usually being played upstage, and therefore further away from the audience than Stoppard's text, and because it is presented as a series of disconnected fragments. Polonius exits, leaving Ros and Guil to make head or tail of Hamlet. He is unable to tell his 'good friends' apart, which continues the tease about fluid identity. Levin makes an interesting comment on Shakespeare's Rosencrantz and Guildenstern:

Their backstage nicknames are the Knife and Fork, partly because they are inseparable, and partly because it is their task to feed Hamlet his lines.

Stoppard plays up the first part of this characterization by making Ros and Guil themselves, as well as the other members of the cast, unable to separate out one part from the other. He plays down the second part of it by witholding the spectacle of Ros and Guil feeding Hamlet his lines. The stage directions in the first edition indicated that part of the conversation between Hamlet and his supposed friends ought to be conveyed through mime. *Hamlet* is reduced, once again, to a dumb show. This is all part of the game of ambushing audiences. Spectators who may not know *Hamlet* well could be forgiven for thinking that this encounter will at last provide some of the answers that Ros and Guil have been seeking. Those who do know it well could point out that, if this encounter was played out in full, it would provide answers which Stoppard wished to ignore. The attendant lords are shown to be clearly implicated in Claudius's web of intrigue rather than just innocent victims of it. The encounter ought to represent a climax. The old tease brings his audience to this potentially high point and then keeps them waiting. He ends the first act, as he began it, with questions rather than answers.

2. Acting Naturally

Weather reports (pp. 40–43)

The second act does not begin where the first one left off. It picks up the encounter towards the end. The dialogue is meant to be '*indecipherable*' (p. 40) at first. One of the consequences of this severe editing is to make Ros and Guil appear to be quite effective questioners. Guil is shown to get one question in, whereas Hamlet is not seen to ask them anything. This sets up the possibilities for the comic fall. It is indeed quite a fall:

ROS: . . . He was scoring off us all down the line.
GUIL: He caught us on the wrong foot once or twice, perhaps, but I thought we gained some ground.
ROS (*simply*):   He murdered us.
GUIL: He might have had the edge.
ROS: Twenty-seven–three, and you think he might have had the edge?! He *murdered* us.   (p. 41)

Guil marshals his packed verbal defence like a canny football manager being interviewed after his team has suffered a particularly humiliating defeat. Ros's version of events is the more accurate one since Shakespeare's text reveals that Hamlet slotted in twenty-seven questions to their three. Like the Carling Black Label commercial, *Rosencrantz* juxtaposes Shakespearian language with football-speak. Such a clash is a familiar one in contemporary comedy. An early Terry Jones and Michael Palin sketch offers a history lesson on the Battle of Hastings. This is described in terms of a journalistic report on a football match rather than in the academic terms which are normally used.

Ros continues to rub in the extent of their humiliation. He also provides another one of his summaries:

ROS: Denmark's a prison and he'd rather live in a nutshell; some shadow-play about the nature of ambition, which never got down to cases, and finally one direct question which might have led somewhere, and led in fact to his illuminating claim to tell a hawk from a handsaw. (*Pause.*)
GUIL: When the wind is southerly.   (p. 42)

It is on the cards that Guil will try to make something of the 'a hawk from a handsaw' reference. He has already shown an interest in flying monkeys, unicorns and the landing habits of bright-feathered birds.

Hamlet's riddle is a good one with which to pass the time. Is 'handsaw' really a corruption of hernshaw or heron? Are both 'hawk' and 'handsaw' terms for tools used in the building trade? The reference, whichever way it is interpreted, points clearly to the fact that Hamlet recognizes his friends as his real enemies. Guil focuses his attention on the direction of the wind, which is not the part of the riddle which usually troubles Shakespearian editors. It becomes for Guil, however, another curious phenomenon. The attendant lords have just had a humiliating interview with Hamlet. Although matters of state may rest on its outcome, they end up talking about the weather. Large, public talk bewilders them, whereas small, private talk sustains them.

The fact that Guil concerns himself with the direction of the wind rather than with Hamlet's meaning is a good joke for the joke's sake. This is also related, however, to the examination of theatricality. There is no weather in an indoor theatre. There may be elemental passions but no elements. All attempts to represent the weather must therefore be highly artificial ones. Ronald Harwood's play *The Dresser* (1980) affectionately parodies the attempts by a touring Shakespearian company during the Second World War to disguise this artificiality with naturalistic sound effects. While 'Sir', the actor-manager, gives the storm scene from *King Lear* everything he has got on stage, all hands man the thunder sheet and the wind machine backstage. The Ghost in *Hamlet* is usually accompanied by a mighty, rushing wind. Less old-fashioned productions prefer to dispense with the pretence of naturalism altogether, relying on words and gestures to represent the elements. This is much truer to the spirit of Shakespearian theatre.

Guil refers to the wind at the end of his filibuster on the law of probability. He claims to have heard the sound of the band 'for the last three minutes on the wind of a windless day' (p. 14). The theatre is not concerned with probability or naturalism, Stoppard suggests, but with artificiality and theatricality. Guil's fascination with the direction of the wind leads to a more sustained revelation of the fact it is always 'windless' in the theatre:

GUIL: I'm trying to establish the direction of the wind.

ROS: There isn't any wind. *Draught*, yes.

GUIL: In that case, the origin. Trace it to its source and it might give us a rough idea of the way we came in – which might give us a rough idea of south, for further reference.

ROS: It's coming up through the floor. (*He studies the floor.*) That can't be south, can it?

GUIL: That's not a direction. Lick your toe and wave it around a bit.   (p. 43)

This attempt to establish both the direction of the wind and a more general sense of direction degenerates into absurdity. This is inevitable because it began on what Stoppard takes to be a false premise: that the theatrical world ought to correspond to the real world. Ros and Guil end up discussing the stage as a stage, or just a floor. They draw attention to the familiar complaint by actors that stages are draughty places. Spectators have also been known to complain about draughty theatres, so this discussion of the weather is designed to make them feel self-conscious about their roles.

It might pass the time to consider some of the other references to the weather in *Rosencrantz*. There is a brief discussion of which direction is east after the attendant lords wake up after the performance of *The Murder of Gonzago*. Ros and Guil discuss the coming of autumn to pass the time before they embark for England. This is another of Guil's speeches which has been taken out of its dramatic context and described as being genuinely poetic. Yet it contains a series of lighting cues and its descriptive language, for instance 'ochres' and 'umber', sounds like that of a theatrical production team straining too hard for special effects. Guil's speech is therefore a parody of theatrical clichés:

Autumnal – nothing to do with leaves. It is to do with a certain brownness at the edges of the day ... Brown is creeping up on us, take my word for it ... Russets and tangerine shades of old gold flushing the very outside edge of the senses ... deep shining ochres, burnt umber and parchments of baked earth – reflecting on itself and through itself, filtering the light. At such times, perhaps, coincidentally, the leaves might fall, somewhere, by repute. Yesterday was blue, like smoke.
(p. 69)

Leaves fall and the wind blows only in somewhere known as the real world. There are more opportunities to discuss the weather when Ros, Guil and Hamlet embark for England. The attendant lords try to work out whether it is night or day. They are also shown to lack knowledge of their nautical direction, just as they are unsure of their theatrical direction. The sea is supposed to be rough and Ros is sick over the side of the boat. The wind is supposed to be strong, which is why, when Hamlet spits into it, he gets one back in the eye almost immediately. All this is one in the eye for spectators who like thunder sheets, wind machines and other naturalistic devices. The representation of Hamlet with spit in his eye continues the process of deflating the Shakespearian hero. It is broadly equivalent to putting a moustache on the *Mona Lisa*.

Acting naturally (pp. 43–51)

Ros and Guil are left high and dry with nothing to write home about after their unsuccessful attempt to locate the direction of south. So they try to provoke the Danish court into making another appearance. Ros urges Guil to 'Give them a shout. Something provocative. *Intrigue* them' (p. 43). The actor–spectator coin is being flipped over again. The actors in *Hamlet*, instead of intriguing the spectators, have to be intrigued by these two on-stage spectators before they will make an entrance. The coin is spun over again as Ros, in his role as actor, confronts the theatre audience for want of anything better to do. He bellows 'Fire!' (p. 44) at the audience but gets no response. The spectators sit still, which is of course what Ros and Guil spend a great deal of the play doing.

Nothing to be done but to play a guessing game with the coins. It is at this point that some of the other actors from *Hamlet* make their entrance. They never appear when they are wanted. Hamlet arranges for *The Murder of Gonzago* to be played by the Tragedians and instructs the Player to incorporate a new speech into it. Rosencrantz and Guildenstern are usually present when Hamlet and Polonius greet the Players. It is indeed they who bring the news that the Players are on their way to Elsinore. It is possible, therefore, for the actor playing Hamlet to indicate his annoyance at the fact that these two attendant lords have missed their cue. They never appear when they are wanted. Hamlet certainly exits with only the briefest acknowledgement of the fact that the 'good lads' are on stage. Ros and Guil decide to work off their frustrations on the Player. Their patronizing attitude towards this performer draws attention to the ways in which spectators, and more particularly reviewers, treat common players. Their tone is cruel, haughty and facetious. They are obviously trying to act the parts of gentlemen who have influence yet at court. Inexperienced actors take it upon themselves to patronize a more experienced one.

The Player feels humiliated because he and his troupe were left to perform their peep-show by the wayside without any spectators peeping at it. The actors are forced to become their own spectators. The Player confronts both Ros and Guil and the theatre audience, which also missed the performance:

... Think, in your head, *now*, think of the most ... *private* ... *secret* ... *intimate* thing you have ever done secure in the knowledge of its privacy ... (*He gives them – and the audience – a good pause.* ROS *takes on a shifty look.*) Are you thinking of it? (*He strikes with his voice and his head.*) Well, I saw you do it! (ROS *leaps up, dissembling madly.*) (p. 46)

Humiliation and embarrassment are transferred to Ros and the theatre audience. The spectator may have the power to give an actor his identity, but then the actor can use his power to challenge the spectator's identity. It is ironic that this histrionic speech, occasioned by the absence of an audience, is self-consciously delivered to such a self-conscious on-stage one. The dramatic context suggests a variation on this ironic theme. Hamlet is probably delivering his 'O, what a rogue and peasant slave am I' (II.2.547) soliloquy, which concerns differences between theatrical and real performance, without an audience. If this performance is not being witnessed, is it really happening? Hamlet and the other members of the Danish court must be mad because they spend a lot of time talking, or performing, to themselves.

The Player dramatically recreates the dramatic non-event. Although Ros and members of the theatre audience may be embarrassed by this performance, Guil continues to play the part of a spectator who is unmoved by it. He claps slowly when it is over with, as the stage directions indicate, '*measured irony*' (p. 47). He then proceeds to review the performance with the same measured irony:

Brilliantly re-created – if these eyes could weep! . . . Rather strong on metaphor, mind you. No criticism – only a matter of taste. And so here you are – with a vengeance. That's a figure of speech . . . isn't it? Well let's say we've made up for it, for you may have no doubt whom to thank for your performance at the court.
(p. 47)

The Player is nevertheless able to reassert his authority simply because he has 'been here before' (p. 48). He is the old pro whereas Ros and Guil, despite all their affectations, do not know whether they are supposed to be making entrances or exits.

Guil's flippant performance suddenly flips over. The Player, acting the nursemaid, attempts to calm him down by dishing out familiar backstage hints for nervous, inexperienced actors:

PLAYER: Relax. Respond. That's what people do. You can't go through life questioning your situation at every turn.
GUIL: But we don't know what's going on, or what to do with ourselves. We don't know how to *act*.
PLAYER: Act natural.
(pp. 48–9)

'Act natural' is the potential contradiction in terms which Stoppard explores throughout *Rosencrantz*. The Player acts naturally because he is always in costume and will only reluctantly leave the stage to make anything as artificial as an entrance. Yet his bombastic and histrionic style of acting is anything but natural. It would not recognize the top if it was perched on it. His advice to Guil is therefore paradoxical. As indicated, Stoppard suggests that the theatre has nothing to do with natural phenomena such as the weather. Despite the Player's advice to behave like real people do, the theatre may also have nothing to do with real people. As he himself puts it earlier on, actors are 'the opposite of people' (p. 46). Stoppard's playful paradox may be that the further over the top an actor goes, the closer he gets to acting naturally. Heightened artificiality and theatricality are, or ought to be, natural phenomena in the theatre.

Ros and more particularly Guil have lost their momentum again. Their game with the Player has turned serious. They therefore have to find another way of passing the time. They return to a game of questions about Hamlet, allowing the Player to feed them some of the lines. Ros finally works out that Hamlet must be 'stark raving sane' (p. 50). This game, like the others that have preceded it, becomes an end in itself and does not lead to any serious conclusions about how to deal with Hamlet. It is, as indicated, being played to postpone such conclusions. The Player leaves to learn the new lines that Hamlet has written for *The Murder of Gonzago*. The old pro does not, however, set an example to the inexperienced actors. Ros even shouts 'Next!' (p. 50), mocking the practice of theatrical auditions, after he has gone. This harks back to the moment during the first act when Guil invokes the clichés of the audition by remarking to Alfred that 'we'll let you know' (p. 25). The fact that such inexperienced performers set themselves up as patrons raises a number of playful questions about the theatre: who auditions the auditioner, reviews the reviewer and directs the director? The more important question that is being posed whenever the Player is on stage concerns who is acting naturally.

The theatrical box (pp. 51–3)

Ros raises the question of death, ironically enough, to pass the time: 'Do you ever think of yourself as actually *dead*, lying in a box with a lid on it?' (p. 51). Stoppard is playing with a coin which has a coffin on one side and a theatre on the other. The stage itself is a box with a draughty bottom and three walls. The fourth wall is missing to allow an audience to watch what is going on, or in this particular case what is not going on. Thus the audience is often referred to in theatrical jargon as the fourth wall. The Player argued that acting without this fourth wall, or open lid, was like dying a death. Ros thinks along the same lines, although his particular version of death is being on stage without directions:

... I'm going to stuff you in this box now, would you rather be alive or dead? Naturally, you'd prefer to be alive. Life in a box is better than no life at all, I expect. You'd have a chance at least. You could lie there thinking – well, at least I'm not dead! In a minute someone's going to bang on the lid and tell me to come out. (*Banging on the floor with his fists.*) 'Hey you, whatsyername! Come out of there!' (pp. 51–2)

There are two related ways of interpreting this speech. First of all, it recreates Ros and Guil's summons by the messenger. He woke them up by banging on their shutters and was ambiguous about names. He gave them the only existence that they can remember. They have no existence as real people but only as actors called to play particular parts. If this messenger is seen as the writer, then this speech provides another example of the way in which Stoppard gives the impression that the author has abandoned them on stage. They are left waiting for their own particular Godot, the God-like omniscient author. Secondly, they are waiting for some sort of direction from the other members of the *Hamlet* cast. These actors are also vague about names and have so far provided nothing equivalent to 'Come out of there!', which can be read as advice about when Ros and Guil should come on and come off the stage. They get no directions from either the writer or the other actors. They also get no response from the spectators when they confront them. If the spectators do not exist, then neither do the actors. It is misleading to describe *Rosencrantz* as a play about death. Leaves fall somewhere else, by repute. Stoppard's theatre is about nothing else but itself.

Ros is, ironically, attempting to cheer Guil up by discussing theatrical death. Stoppard clashes the idioms by framing some of Ros's more haunting observations within a cabaret act complete with appalling Jewish jokes. There is another kind of clash being effected since the subject matter is pure Guil, although it is delivered by Ros:

... Whatever became of the moment when one first knew about death? There must have been one, a moment, in childhood when it first occurred to you that you don't go on for ever. It must have been shattering – stamped into one's memory. And yet I can't remember it. It never occurred to me at all. (p. 52)

Stoppard may be spinning the coin which has Ros on one side and Guil on the other. It is just as likely, however, that Ros is choosing the kind of subjects which he knows will interest Guil. You have to find something to talk about if you are trapped in a theatrical box.

The direct informal approach (pp. 53–5)

Ros is unable to prolong this particular filibuster against silence. If the other actors refuse to 'come out talking' (p. 52), he is going to 'forbid anyone to enter' (p. 53). This provides the cue for Claudius, Gertrude, Polonius and others to process on. The attendant lords are, once again, ambushed by theatrical events beyond their control. The stage directions give an impression of the ensuing confusion:

CLAUDIUS *takes* ROS*'s elbow as he passes and is immediately deep in conversation* ... GUIL *still faces front as* CLAUDIUS, ROS, *etc. pass upstage and turn* ... *He turns upstage in time to take over the conversation with* CLAUDIUS. (p. 53)

Guil in fact just has time to deliver the piece of graffiti about 'Death followed by eternity' being 'the worst of both worlds' before he plunges himself into his Shakespearian part. Stoppard teases the theatre audience by converting the beginning of this scene from *Hamlet* into another dumb show. The stage directions do not spell out how Claudius reacts to the presence of Ros and Guil on stage when they are meant to be bringing up the rear of his procession. Perhaps he grabs hold of Ros to make sure that he does not cause any more trouble. After the dumb show with Claudius, Ros and Guil are questioned by Gertrude. Shakespeare's play, which is reduced to being one of the plays within Stoppard's play, produces some unintentionally funny lines. Ros puts a brave face on their defeat by Hamlet, whom he declares to have been 'Niggard of question, but of our demands most free in his reply' (p. 53). Acting naturally involves lying.

Ros and Guil's idiomatic language does not fall apart after this second brief encounter with the Danish court. They are able to wheel out their clichés as soon as the procession wheels off. They need to have them ready and waiting for when Hamlet appears upstage. His famous 'To be, or not to be' (III.1.56) soliloquy is reduced to mime. Ros offers the theatre audience a parody of it with his 'To accost, or not to accost' speech with its medley of modern clichés:

Nevertheless, I suppose one might say this was a chance ... One might well ... accost him ... Yes, it definitely looks like a chance to me ... Something on the lines of a direct informal approach ... man to man ... straight from the shoulder ... Now look here, what's it all about ... sort of thing. Yes. Yes, this looks like one to be grabbed with both hands, I should say . . . if I were asked . . . No point in looking at a gift horse till you see the whites of its eyes, etcetera.   (pp. 54–5)

Ros predictably enough loses his nerve and fails to accost the great man. The contrast between the idiomatic and the Shakespearian is rounded off perfectly when Hamlet breaks off his soliloquy to accost Ophelia, who, according to Stoppard, enters as part of a religious procession. His greeting to her, with its classical and religious associations, is hardly a direct, informal approach: 'Nymph, in thy orisons be all my sins remembered' (p. 55).

Dumb shows (pp. 55–64)

Ros's failure at the direct, informal approach means that it is now his turn to flip over. His manic confidence gives way to depression. Guil, who has had to be nursemaided through a difficult patch, now resumes his more familiar role as the nursemaid; 'If I might make a suggestion – shut up and sit down. Stop being perverse' (p. 55). Ros does not want to sit around and brood. His only way of fighting back both tears and depression is to try to fight against this kind of inactivity. He therefore goes up behind a female figure who has just appeared on stage and accosts her. He does so in a manner reminiscent of childhood games: putting his hands over her eyes and asking her to play a guessing game. The figure turns out to be neither Gertruden nor Ophelia, but Alfred dressed up to play the woman's part in *The Murder of Gonzago*. Ros's decisive bid for action therefore rebounds on itself. His question, 'Guess who?!' (p. 55), becomes a double-edged one. He has always been unsure of his own identity and does not know the identity of his new playmate. Despite his attempts to convince himself that he had no interest in peepshows, he hankered after a performance either from or with Alfred. This encounter therefore takes the form of wish-fulfilment. It is not, however, set within a pleasurable dream. The menacing entry of the Player and the Tragedians suggests that he is trapped in a nightmare. He is also still trapped within the theatrical box, although his breezy acceptance of this position has now given way to a frightened pessimism about it.

The idea of the Tragedians having a dress rehearsal is ironic since they are almost always in costume anyway. It nevertheless provides the opportunity for a further exploration of theatricality. The Player, whose numerous parts have already included a theatrical impresario and an angry actor, now casts himself as a theatrical director. He begins this performance with mannered witticisms:

Stop picking your nose, Alfred. When Queens have to they do it by a cerebral process passed down in the blood . . . (p. 56)

His tone becomes more petulant: 'No, no, no! Dumbshow first, your confounded majesty' (p. 56). The dumb show eventually gets under way. Despite their theatrical pretensions, Ros and Guil have to have even the simplest things explained to them:

GUIL: What is the dumbshow for?
PLAYER: Well, it's a device, really – it makes the action that follows more or less comprehensible; you understand, we are tied down to a language which makes up in obscurity what it lacks in style. (pp. 56–7)

Stoppard parodies the kind of avant-garde director who believes that actions speak louder than words. Such a position is undermined when the Player is forced to supply a running commentary on the dumb show for Ros and Guil's benefit.

The dumb show is suddenly interrupted by the appearance of Hamlet and Ophelia. Stoppard teases his spectators by plunging them into the final moments of the nunnery scene. He also denies them an opportunity to hear Ophelia's famous speech on the decline of the Renaissance ideal: 'O, what a noble mind is here o'erthrown!' (III.1.151). After Hamlet exits, Ophelia merely falls on her knees for a quiet cry. Her speech, like Hamlet's 'To be, or not to be' soliloquy is reduced to a dumb show. The tease is continued by the way in which Stoppard includes a prosaic speech by Claudius at the expense of Ophelia's more poetic one. Claudius begins to outline his plot to send Hamlet to England, but then leaves the stage in the middle of the speech. Now you see, and more occasionally hear, the members of the Danish court, now you don't.

Stoppard's spectators have been watching a rehearsal for the dumb show which will precede the performance of *The Murder of Gonzago* at the court. *Gonzago* is the play within the play of *Hamlet*, which is in its turn the play within the play of *Rosencrantz*. Nothing succeeds like excess in Stoppard's theatrical games. Matters are complicated still further by the fact that the actor–spectator coin is being flipped over again. The Tragedians freeze in the attitude of an audience when Hamlet enters. Yet he treats them as performers by delivering his lines against marriage to the Tragedians who represent Claudius and Gertrude. There is therefore another coin spinning up in the air with rehearsal on one side and performance on the other.

The Player attempts to get his show back on the proverbial road after this interruption. Confusion is still the name of the game as Ros believes

that the Player is commenting on, and therefore directing, the performance from *Hamlet* as well:

PLAYER: Gentlemen! It doesn't seem to be coming. We are not getting it at all.
   (*To* GUIL) What did you think?
GUIL: What was I supposed to think?
PLAYER (*to* TRAGEDIANS): You're not getting across!
   (ROS *had gone half way up to* OPHELIA; *he returns*.)
ROS: That didn't look like love to me.   (p. 58)

Stoppard pulls one of the biggest rabbits out of his hat by giving the
impression that *Hamlet* might be the play within the play of *The Murder
of Gonzago*.

   The Player carries on trying to direct the rehearsal in his usual medley
of voices. He plays the music hall comedian raising a quick laugh:

PLAYER: ... My goodness no – over your dead body.
GUIL: How am I supposed to take that?
PLAYER: Lying down.   (p. 58)

He drops the part of the avant-garde director in favour of one of a brisk,
no nonsense man of the theatre:

We're tragedians, you see. We follow directions – there is no *choice* involved.
The bad end unhappily, the good unluckily. That is what tragedy means.   (p. 59)

The breezy clichés, adapted from Oscar Wilde, only heighten Guil's
impotent anger. He has become interested in the insoluble problem of
accident and design again. Ros's frustrations are less metaphysical and
more physical. The passionate nature of the dumb show, heightened by
the Player's unnecessary running commentary on it, provokes another of
his outbursts against sexually explicit theatre. Like Hamlet, both Ros
and Guil offer advice to the Players:

ROS: Well, really – I mean, people want to be *entertained* – they don't come
   expecting sordid and gratuitous filth.
PLAYER: You're wrong – they do! Murder, seduction and incest – what do you
   want – *jokes*?
ROS: I want a good story, with a beginning, middle and end.
PLAYER (to GUIL):   And you?
GUIL: I'd prefer art to mirror life, if it's all the same to you.
PLAYER: It's all the same to me, sir.   (p. 59)

They are reviewing *Rosencrantz* as well as *The Murder of Gonzago*.
Stoppard's play contains jokes about 'Murder, seduction and incest'

rather than a detailed treatment of them. Its circular nature gives the impression that it does not have 'a beginning, middle and end'. It holds its mirror up to 'art' rather than to 'life'. Guil's advice is close to Hamlet's:

... For anything so o'erdone is from the purpose of playing, whose end, both at the first and now, was and is to hold, as 'twere, the mirror up to nature, to show virtue her own feature, scorn her own image, and the very age and body of the time his form and pressure.   (III.2.19–24)

The parody of the main themes of *Hamlet* continues throughout *Rosencrantz* and is not just confined to those moments when the Danish court is on stage. Guil puts Hamlet's advice into shorthand while retaining its essence. There is, however, a difference as far as reception is concerned. Hamlet delivers his advice to a captive audience of players. The First Player only makes two short, deferential responses to it. Shakespeare's irony is that Hamlet preaches understatement while practising overstatement. Guil's advice, by contrast, is received with a cheeky, mock-deference by the Player. Stoppard's players, unlike Shakespeare's, backchat the gentlemen. University students are not allowed to have the last word about the theatre. Acting naturally may, paradoxically, involve overstatement.

The Player now adds the part of Lucianus, the Hamlet figure, to his repertoire. He not only plays this part but is also able to stand outside his performance and offer a running commentary on it. He is, at one and the same time, both an actor and a spectator. The actor–spectator relationship is then examined from a different angle. Stoppard's dumb show, unlike Shakespeare's, includes an unflattering representation of Ros and Guil, who continue to provide the on-stage audience for the rehearsal. They watch the actors who are representing them depart by ship for England, meet the king and receive their sentences of death. The Player refuses to say whether this death warrant is the result of accident or design: 'Traitors hoist by their own petard? – or victims of the gods? – we shall never know!' (p. 61). Ros stages his own kind of dumb show by his dumb and uncomprehending reaction to these events. The spectator warily approaches the actor who has been representing him. He believes that he has mistaken the identity of the actor although, ironically, it is in fact one of the few occasions in the play when he is not mistaken about identity:

Well, if it isn't – ! No, wait a minute, don't tell me – it's a long time since – where was it? Ah, this is taking me back to – when was it? I know you, don't I? I never forget a face –   (p. 61)

Ros is playing a game of 'guess who?' with his double and he still gets the answer wrong. His string of clichés are, once again. a source of comfort in a bewildering situation.

Ros and Guil are unable to concentrate on specifics. It does not matter whether the subject is how to handle Hamlet, or what to make of these two doubles in the dumb show. Just as the form of their conversations consists largely of clichés, so they prefer the content of them to remain as general as possible. They therefore discuss the concept of theatrical death in general. Ironically, their doubles have to wait around, sentenced to death, while this particular red herring is pursued. The Player tells Ros and Guil a story:

> ... I had an actor once who was condemned to hang for stealing a sheep – or a lamb, I forget which – so I got permission to have him hanged in the middle of a play – had to change the plot a bit but I thought it would be effective, you know – and you wouldn't believe it, he just *wasn't* convincing! It was impossible to suspend one's disbelief – and what with the audience jeering and throwing peanuts, the whole thing was a *disaster*! – he did nothing but cry all the time – right out of character – just stood there and cried . . . Never again. (p. 62)

Stoppard's comedy usually operates on a number of different levels. First of all, there is a quick joke for joke's sake with the introduction of the proverbial saying that one might as well be hung for a sheep as for a lamb. Secondly, the passage continues the parody of theatrical directors: 'he just *wasn't* convincing . . . the whole thing was a *disaster*'. Thirdly, Stoppard introduces one of his more caviar jokes with the phrase to 'suspend one's disbelief'. This may have an immediate comic impact in a speech which is about the suspension, or hanging, of a man on stage. Yet the joke also depends on its reference to Coleridge's famous statement on poetic faith in *Biographia Literaria* (1817): 'That willing suspension of disbelief for the moment, which constitutes poetic faith'. Stoppard stands Coleridge on his head as a 'willing suspension of disbelief' should not be necessary if a real event is taking place on stage. Finally, the speech as a whole continues the exploration of theatricality. It shows how spectators become part of the spectacle and raises questions about what acting naturally ought to entail. The integration of different levels of comedy with underlying thematic structures suggests that those critics who accuse Stoppard of just playing around on the surface are themselves being superficial. The comedy in this speech is certainly primarily verbal, but it would again be a superficial reading to suggest that Stoppard is only interested in wordplay. The two Tragedians who represent Ros and

Guil are waiting on stage to be executed. If the Player, as befits such an authoritarian director and histrionic actor, takes the centre of the stage, then the positions of the others can be patterned around him. He might have these two Tragedians on his left and Ros and Guil on his right. Despite the fact that both these groups look remarkably similar, their reactions to the speech will probably be different. The Tragedians' dead-pan expressions should probably contrast with Ros and Guil's more agitated looks and gestures. Indeed, the visual comedy during the Player's speech itself should come mainly from Guil's expressions of dissent. As soon as the speech is over, the two Tragedians are asked to demonstrate convincing theatrical deaths. Their expressions should change quickly and dramatically. Like the Player himself, they should generate some visual comedy by the obvious way in which they switch from role to role, in this case from playing spectators to playing actors. The stage directions earlier on indicate that the Player's smile is switched on and off in a very obvious manner. The two Tragedians take some time staging their convincing theatrical deaths. The verbal comedy of the Player's speech is therefore followed and reinforced by this visual comedy sequence.

Traitors or victims? (pp. 63–70)

The rehearsal–performance coin is flipped over again. The rehearsal at which Ros and Guil have been spectators is also revealed to be the performance which Claudius and the court have been watching. Stoppard's version is that Claudius, unlike Ros and Guil, does not need a running commentary to work out the implications of the dumb show and disrupts it. Stoppard himself may be more concerned to tease rather than alienate his audience but Hamlet, who stages the play within the play, wants to confront and offend Claudius. He stages a thinly veiled representation of Claudius's crime, as well as a warning that it will be revenged. Claudius establishes his guilt by walking out of a play which represents what he thought was his secret. This dramatic exit, when it is re-located within Stoppard's play, continues the game with the theatre audience. It is allowed to glimpse an on-stage audience walking out of a performance.

Stoppard bends Shakespeare's text in order to achieve this neat and effective coming together of the two plays. There has always been a controversy among Shakespearian critics about whether Claudius pays any attention to the dumb show. It is certainly true that he disrupts *The Murder of Gonzago* itself rather than the dumb show which precedes it.

This point does not, however, have a substantial bearing on readings of Stoppard's play. This is not the case with the way in which the Shakespearian text is used after the dumb show has been disrupted. Stoppard picks up the action with the confusion that surrounds the murder of Polonius rather than with that which, specifically, follows on from Claudius's exit. He therefore omits altogether the two scenes which show that Rosencrantz and Guildenstern are not innocents abroad but somewhat clumsy participants in Claudius's web of intrigue and deception. They are sent by Gertrude with the message that Hamlet must come and see her. Hamlet mocks their attempts to play the parts of courtiers by exaggerating both their mode of address and the gestures that accompany it. Guildenstern begs him to stop this parody of them: 'Nay, good my lord, this courtesy is not of the right breed' (III.2.321–2). The statement is ironic since, as Hamlet delights in demonstrating, it is these two attendant lords who affect a courtly breeding which they do not in fact possess. They deliver their message and then seek to confirm their hypothesis that Hamlet's behaviour is explained by his thwarted ambition. These two ambitious courtiers, who hope for advancement by doing Claudius's dirty work for him, can only see Hamlet as a reflection of themselves. It is open to question as to whether Hamlet acts out of political ambition. He may allow Rosencrantz and Guildenstern to believe that this is the case, but only to stop them probing into the events surrounding the appearance of the Ghost. Rosencrantz reveals that, despite his relatively late arrival at Elsinore, he is well aware of the political situation there. He asks Hamlet why he is ambitious when he has 'the voice of the King himself for your succession in Denmark' (III.2.349–50). One of the Players interrupts this cross-examination by bringing Hamlet the recorders for which he has sent. He uses Guildenstern's lack of musical ability to parallel a lack of political subtlety and ability:

... You would play upon me. You would seem to know my stops. You would pluck out the heart of my mystery. You would sound me from my lowest note to the top of my compass. And there is much music, excellent voice, in this little organ. Yet cannot you make it speak. 'Sblood, do you think I am easier to be played on than a pipe? Call me what instrument you will, though you can fret me, you cannot play upon me.   (III.2.372–9)

This scene leaves little doubt that Rosencrantz and Guildenstern are knowingly implicated in Claudius's surveillance of Hamlet. Shakespeare represents them as betrayers of, and traitors to, their friendship with Hamlet rather than as innocent victims of courtly intrigue.

Shakespeare then shows Rosencrantz and Guildenstern being briefed by Claudius about the need to take Hamlet to England. They both attempt to flatter Claudius and yet end up unwittingly representing him as a tyrant. Guildenstern declares that

> . . . Most holy and religious fear it is
> To keep those many many bodies safe
> That live and feed upon your majesty.

(III.3.8–10)

The intention may be to pay homage to the idea that the king rules by divine right, although the sharpest image of Claudius that emerges is as a carcass that attracts parasites. Similarly, Rosencrantz sycophantically runs through a number of Elizabethan clichés about relationships between monarchs and subjects, yet perverts their emphasis on harmony and balance with his own stress on strength. As will become more apparent during the detailed analysis of *Hamlet* later on, Stoppard's omission of these scenes is part of a wider attempt to depoliticize Shakespeare's text.

Stoppard only jumps back into *Hamlet* at the point when Claudius urges Ros and Guil to track down Hamlet after the murder of Polonius. They are, however, incapable of acting upon summonses or commands. They strut around the stage fretting about what might happen to them if they leave it and each other. They are still trapped in the box. The irony is that their frenzied activity is just another form of inactivity. They catch sight of Hamlet off-stage and decide to trap him. The trapped decide to become the trappers. Hamlet is too good at hide-and-seek for them. He eludes their clumsy grasp. Ros's trousers elude him for a while. Hamlet saunters on to the stage: now you see him, now you don't. He attempts to dress down Ros and Guil for being Claudius's agents. His scorn is wasted, however, since these two can only ever act dumb. They do not soak up the metaphor about the sponge, which ironically seems to disprove Hamlet's analysis. Hamlet's footwork, literally and metaphorically, is much too fast for them. Like two clumsy full-backs, they try to sandwich this star forward player. He just sells the dummies a clever little dummy. Ros and Guil are thus caught very flat-footed when Claudius returns, expecting his wish to have been their command. They bluff it out and the unexpected return of Hamlet allows them to pluck victory from the jaws of defeat. Shakespeare's attendant lords are in charge of the palace guard, while Stoppard's ones act independently of it. This provides another example of Stoppard's special pleading for them. He also omits Claudius's last-minute instructions to them for the journey to England. They therefore set off with little understanding of their mission. Ros assures the theatre audience that 'anything could happen yet' (p. 70). How long, oh attendant lords, how long before anything happens at all?

3. Theatrical Life on the Ocean Wave

Carry on cruising (pp. 71–6)

Act Three opens in pitch darkness. The audience might be listening to a radio play. The action might be taking place at sea. Stoppard ambushes naturalistic sound effects as part of the general ambush of naturalistic theatre. He offers a list of nautical cries and then adds, teasingly, that they ought to be continued until *'the point has been well made and more so'* (p. 72). The voices of the jolly tars, which are established against background sounds of shivering timbers and heaving hearties, become comically absurd rather than naturalistically authentic. This is easy enough to achieve with some gems as 'Hard a larboard' and 'Tops'l up, me maties' (p. 72). The tops'l only goes up somewhere else by repute, which is why Stoppard insists that such cries should be allowed to go over the top. Radio comedy is stuffed with similar parodies of sound effects. The *I'm Sorry I'll Read That Again* team did a good send-up of theatrical life on the ocean wave in a play called *Search for the Nile*. Their cries included 'Belay there ye swabs' and 'Stand to ye lubbers'. It was also a good opportunity for the Long John Silver impersonators to get in on the act. Stoppard's parody provides similar opportunities for those who feel at home with such rolling, deep accents. The comedy is reinforced by the way in which Ros eventually makes the brilliant deduction from these sound effects that 'We're on a boat' (p. 72).

More light is shed on their predicament. It reveals that Hamlet is sitting upstage under *'a gaudy striped umbrella . . . one of those huge six-foot diameter jobs'* (pp. 72–3). The characters have been dressed throughout the play in rather shabby Elizabethan costumes. Props have been kept to a minimum, although they should also appear to be authentic period ones. This carefully cultivated authenticity is thrown overboard with the appearance of the modern striped umbrella. Just as Shakespearian and modern language clash throughout the play, so now there is an opposition between Elizabethan props and modern ones. Period atmosphere is therefore shown to be just as contrived and artificial as nautical atmosphere.

Stoppard continues this ambush of naturalism when Ros is sick over the side of the boat. Ros affects to look out over the sea, although he is in fact looking at the sea of faces which make up the audience. Just one look is enough for him. Stoppard's introduction of sea-sickness at all may be related to the way in which he continually juxtaposes the prosaic with the poetic. Sea-sickness and dormant mice are not the stuff of Shakespearian tragedy.

Ros and Guil are metaphorically at sea as well. Guil nevertheless attempts to make virtues out of their necessities. He likes messing about in boats because they represent 'safe areas in a game of tag' (p. 73). Guil the child feels comfortable, as he tries to explain while Ros is feeling distinctly uncomfortable over the side of the boat:

Free to move, speak, extemporise, and yet. We have not been cut loose. Our truancy is defined by one fixed star, and our drift represents merely a slight change of angle to it: we may seize the moment, toss it around while the moments pass, a short dash here, an exploration there, but we are brought round full circle to face again the single immutable fact – that we, Rosencrantz and Guildenstern, bearing a letter from one king to another, are taking Hamlet to England. (p. 74)

The fact that Ros is being sick upstage does not provide a suitably heroic context for this soliloquy. It might even suggest that all soliloquies are theatrical padding, which is of course another way of devaluing *Hamlet*. Guil is also made to undermine this attempt to grasp at significant straws by the familiar clash between Shakespearian and modern idioms.

His reference to the fact that Hamlet is also a passenger deflates Ros's attempt to make a dramatic announcement of the news. Ros is unable to remember what happened at the end of the last act. Guil has a better understanding of the situation and it is this which makes him more prone to anger and frustration. So Ros tries to cheer him up by playing the 'guess which hand' game with the coins. The double act eventually has to review itself for want of anything better to do:

GUIL: Why don't you say something original! No wonder the whole thing is so stagnant! You don't take me up on anything – you just repeat it in a different order.
ROS: I can't think of anything original. I'm only good in support.
GUIL: I'm sick of making the running.
ROS (*Humbly*): It must be your dominant personality. (*Almost in tears*) Oh, what's going to become of us!
(*And* GUIL *comforts him, all harshness gone.*) (p. 76)

Ros and Guil are forced to have a conversation about conversation, which both reviews itself and the play of which it is a part. Guil's bid to give up making the 'running' may suggest character development, but then he immediately drops back into his familiar role of nursemaid. Ros and Guil do not develop as characters. They change only in the sense that they alternate between a number of limited roles.

Playing the king (pp. 76–82)

Guil comforts both himself and Ros with the fact that the letter from Claudius to the English king will explain everything. Like the Player, he believes that it is necessary to accept what is written. This is also, incidentally, the position towards which Shakespeare's Hamlet moves with his increasing acceptance of 'providence' (V.2.214). Ros and Guil are, predictably enough, unable to remember where they put this letter, although when they eventually find it it becomes a talisman to ward off the evil of uncertainty. It now becomes Ros's turn to resent his position of stooge or feed in the double-act. If everything is written, then he will have even less room for manoeuvre. If he jumps over the side of the boat, he may merely be doing what has been written down for him to do. He comes to accept the position of the Player and Guildenstern: 'We don't question, we don't doubt. We perform' (p. 79). Yet his anger at having to do so fuels his performance as the English king. He leaps for once straight into a new game without having to be given a laborious summary of the rules. The double-act reverses itself as he makes the running and Guil is barely able to get a word in edgeways:

ROS: And who are you?
GUIL: We are Rosencrantz and Guildenstern.
ROS: Never heard of you!
GUIL: Well, we're nobody special –
ROS: What's your game?   (p. 79)

Ros snatches the sealed letter from Guil, tears it open and begins to read it out. A game has at last provided an explanation of what is written rather than petering out into questions or doubts:

I see . . . I see . . . well, this seems to support your story such as it is – it is an exact command from the King of Denmark, for several different reasons, importing Denmark's health and England's too, that on the reading of this letter, without delay, I should have Hamlet's head cut off – !   (p. 80)

Stoppard borrows his wording of this letter from Hamlet's description of it to Horatio (V.2.19–21). The discovery of the contents of the letter appears to mean that Ros and Guil are now in a position to control their destinies rather than being controlled by the plot of *Hamlet*. Ironically, their questions did not produce this answer. It came through perform-ance, or acting naturally.

Ros's immediate reaction to the discovery suggests that he would rather not have made it. He starts to make conversation about the weather. Guil resumes his role as the dominant partner in the double act. He denies that Hamlet is their friend, which is reasonable on the evidence to date and is confirmed by Hamlet's subsequent actions. The problem here is that Shakespeare wrote that Hamlet was their friend. They are thus back on the slippery slope of questioning and doubting what has been written. Guil produces another one of his filibusters both to cover up an embarrassing silence and to avoid having to deal directly with this problem. His subject is death, which has already been done to death. The shock of the new always sends both Ros and Guil rushing back to the old. Guil puts on his best academic manner for the occasion: 'Well, yes, and then again no' (p. 80). He proceeds to demonstrate, to both the on-stage and theatre audience for this lecture, that Hamlet's death warrant should not be challenged. He leap-frogs through a number of con-tradictory arguments. He argues, first of all, that Hamlet is going to die anyway. There is no answer to this. Secondly, he suggests that the death of Hamlet, one man among many, is not anything to get steamed up about. Thirdly, he puts forward the illogical argument that, because death is not an event in life, it might be a 'very nice' (p. 80) experience. They are therefore doing Hamlet a favour. Finally, and in direct con-tradiction to the point about Hamlet just being one man among many, he suggests that it is not the job of cogs to interfere with big wheels:

... Or to look at it another way – we are little men, we don't know the ins and outs of the matter, there are wheels within wheels, etcetera – it would be presump-tuous of us to interfere with the designs of fate or even of kings. All in all, I think we'd be well advised to leave well alone.   (p. 81)

Ironically, some of the arguments he uses to justify Hamlet's death are precisely those which are used to justify his own. He, more than Hamlet, is just an ordinary person whose death will not cause a great stir. Hamlet himself uses a combination of Guil's first and last points to justify to Horatio why he sent the attendant lords to their deaths:

> 'Tis dangerous when the baser nature comes
> Between the pass and fell incensèd points
> Of mighty opposites.
>
> (V.2.60–63)

The 'mighty opposites' are Hamlet and Claudius. Rosencrantz and Guildenstern can be disposed of without qualms, or 'conscience' (V.2.58), because they have presumed to interfere in this battle of the giants.

It is open to question, and meant to be, whether the discovery of the contents of the letter represents a turning point about which Ros and Guil fail to turn. Some critics believe that they have this opportunity and are therefore guilty of expediency, nihilism and even Fascism by not taking it. Their tragedy is that, when the moment unexpectedly comes, they are unable to think or act independently. This interpretation sees Ros and Guil as modern characters in a modern play. Other critics suggest that Ros and Guil's tragedy is not that they miss opportunities, but rather that there are none to miss. Attendant lords do not have the capacity to think or act independently. Even if Ros and Guil proved that they were an exception to this general rule, they would still find themselves crushed between the 'mighty opposites'. This interpretation tends to see Ros and Guil as being fundamentally Renaissance stereotypes who remain trapped within the framework of a Renaissance play. The problem with both these interpretations is that they are in danger of offering psychological readings of Ros and Guil as if they were real people. Stoppard's theatre of theatre is designed to challenge such readings. Just as he refuses to pretend that the theatre can contain anything approximating to real wind or leaves, so he emphasizes that it can only contain actors who self-consciously play parts. The debate may, however, be translated into these essentially theatrical terms. It then becomes one about whether there is any escape from the part as written. Stoppard's dramatization of this conflict is just one of the ways in which he holds his mirror up to the theatre. This dramatization of conflict may therefore serve a more important function than the resolution to it. As will become more apparent, Stoppard believes, like Hamlet, that actors ought to perform what 'is set down for them' (III.2.38). He would be out of a job if he did not think so. Such a position is open to a variety of political interpretations depending on point of view. The important point to stress is that by writing about writing Stoppard is heightening the theatricality of *Rosencrantz*.

Guil seals up Hamlet's death warrant. Ros attempts to get his bearings straight by offering another summary of the 'story so far', although he admits with comic understatement that some of its 'nuances' have been 'outside our appreciation' (p. 81). He recites this as a comforting bedtime tale. Hamlet, in a distinctly unfriendly gesture, substitutes their death warrant for his own while they are tucked up asleep. Perhaps he would have done exactly the same even if Guil had argued in favour of disclosure rather than discretion. The irony was that, in trying to be discreet, Guil disclosed everything to the eavesdropping Hamlet. This might suggest that attendant lords get jumped on whichever way they jump. Hamlet's long and self-satisfied description of how he made this switch appears to shock even Horatio. His comment on it, 'So Guildenstern and Rosencrantz go to't' (V.2.56), carries a note of reproach which forces Hamlet to stop basking in the glory of the deed and to provide some justification for it. Ros, unaware that Hamlet has pulled this fast one on them, offers another comforting summary when he wakes up. The actor who delivers the explanations is much more ignorant than the spectators who have to listen to them, both because they should have a better general knowledge of events and also because, more specifically, they have just seen Hamlet pull off the switch. The situation is close to pantomime. Ros is blissfully unaware that somebody has crept up behind him in the middle of the night. Should the spectators have shouted out 'Behind you!'? Perhaps they still could. Ros played the part of the king very well and was rewarded with a glimpse of the future. Although Stoppard does not draw the parallel, it should still be noted that he and Guil are out-manoeuvred by somebody who plays the part of a king even better. Hamlet explains to Horatio how he used his father's signet ring to seal up the letter so that the substitution would not be noticed. Ros may play a short-tempered king, but Hamlet plays a more cunning one.

Sustained action (pp. 82–7)

The sound of music offers a welcome relief. This time it is Guil rather than Ros who expresses more interest in it:

> Out of the void, finally, a sound; while on a boat (admittedly) outside the action (admittedly) the perfect and absolute silence of the wet lazy slap of water against water and the rolling creak of timber – breaks; giving rise at once to the speculation or the assumption or the hope that something is about to happen; a pipe is heard.
> (p. 82)

The awkward syntax may represent a parody of either forms of documentary narration or, more particularly, the spoken stage directions from a radio play. It could be, however, that Guil has suddenly woken up to the fact that he is supposed to be playing a German university student. He goes on to mimic the terms in which Hamlet gave him a musical lesson. As indicated, Stoppard does not include this scene so this represents one of his more caviar jokes. Guil affects a musical knowledge which he does not possess and is content to borrow Hamlet's phrases to cover up his ignorance. He has stored away the facts about musicianship in a literal way, but appears to have missed Hamlet's metaphorical implications. Curious phenomena have always interested him more than phenomenal insights.

The music comes from the Tragedians who have stowed away to avoid Claudius's wrath. Now you don't see them, now you do as they emerge from the three barrels that are on the deck. Everybody is now 'in the same boat' (p. 83), according to that barrel of laughs, the Player. The journey has not withered, nor custom staled his infinite variety act:

ROS: Are we all right for England?
PLAYER: You look all right to me. I don't think they're very particular in England.   (p. 84)

The appearance of the Tragedians does not alter the fact that cruises can get rather dull. Ros and Guil have another stab at unravelling the 'story so far'. Ros laments the lack of action:

Incidents! All we get is incidents! Dear God, is it too much to expect a little sustained action?   (p. 86)

He is either taking the words out of the spectators' mouths or putting them there. His previous calls for action or explanation have all been deflated. And now for something completely different – a pirate attack. Stoppard at last provides Ros and the audience with what they want. Tom lad, a literary pirate if ever there was one, lets go the stays, flies the jib and introduces 'a little sustained action'.

A pirate attack is always on the horizon, although it is by no means certain when, if at all, Stoppard will introduce it. The third act of *Rosencrantz*, unlike the first two ones, is much freer in its relationship to the *Hamlet* text. It is, until the finale, based loosely around events that are reported rather than staged and is thus not being continually interrupted by scenes from *Hamlet*. As the structure of parallel performances has been lost, it becomes harder to predict exactly when these reported events will be slotted into Stoppard's play. So, although the attack is referred to by Shakespeare, Stoppard can still ambush his audience by introducing it when he does.

Hamlet's description of the event in his letter to Horatio emphasizes his own swashbuckling part in it:

. . . Ere we were two days old at sea, a pirate of very warlike appointment gave us chase. Finding ourselves too slow of sail, we put on a compelled valour, and in the

grapple I boarded them. On the instant they got clear of our ship. So I alone became
their prisoner. They have dealt with me like thieves of mercy.   (IV.6.15–20)

It seems at first that Stoppard might follow this heroic version of events.
Despite the confused collisions between those under attack, there seems
to be a genuine desire for action. Hamlet himself does not put in an
Errol Flynn performance, although the others might all be challenging
for a place in *The Guinness Book of Records* for how many pirates can be
piled up on a dead man's chest. Yet it rapidly becomes apparent that
Stoppard is parodying stage fights in much the same way as he parodied
theatrical life on the ocean wave: 'At last! To arms! Pirates! Up there!
Down there! To my sword's length! Action!' (pp. 86–7). Ros, Guil,
Hamlet and the Player may rush upstage for a spot of grappling, yet
they beat a hasty, undignified retreat downstage without a blow being
struck. Stoppard strikes a blow against Hamlet's heroic credentials. He
also implies that writers may be liars. Hamlet's account of the pirate
attack is a forgery, as is his letter to the English king. The problem with
accepting what is written is that it may be a pack of lies.

Ros's bluff is called. He hankers after sustained action and then runs
away from the possibility of it. So the pirate attack becomes just another
'incident' through this failure to rise to the occasion. Stoppard ambushes
the audience by appearing to provide something completely different.
He then ambushes the ambush by making this event another of the play's
anti-climaxes. The swashbuckling Stoppard – we seek him up there, we
seek him down there, to his sword's length he attacks us everywhere.

The dance of death (pp. 87–93)

The actors who provided pirate noises steer 'hard a larboard' back to the
dressing-rooms. Stoppard passes the time by playing the three barrel trick
with the audience. One of the three barrels is shown to be missing when
the lights come up after the pirate attack. It appears to be the one into
which Ros and Guil had climbed. Yet they are the first to re-appear. The
Player then emerges from the barrel into which the unheroic Hamlet had
bolted. Stoppard has got his audience over a barrel. Ros and Guil's anxiety over Hamlet's absence leads to another breakdown of their idiomatic
language and the Player has to take over the nursemaid role. Guil is not
to be appeased and his frustrated anger fuels his performance as the English king. The double-act alternates rather than develops. This time it is
Guil rather than Ros who snatches the letter and tears it open. A game
of imaginary conversations leads once more to a glimpse of the future.

Guil is unable to cope with the specific fact that he has seen a copy of his own death warrant, so he responds with a more general discussion of death. The Player and the Tragedians, who have emerged as if by magic from one of the barrels, circle round the attendant lords amid the encircling gloom. Although performance has provided Guil with this glimpse of the future, he nevertheless continues his assault on the theatrical profession:

> . . . I'm talking about death – and you've never experienced *that*. And you cannot *act* it. You die a thousand casual deaths – with none of that intensity which squeezes out life . . . and no blood runs cold anywhere. Because even as you die you know that you will come back in a different hat. But no one gets up after *death* – there is no applause – there is only silence and some second-hand clothes, and that's – *death* – (p. 90)

He stabs the Player. He has taken matters into his own hands for the first time. Perhaps his tragedy really is that he did not do so before. Stoppard lies in wait to ambush such interpretations. It is, of course, easy enough to pick up the clues as to what might happen next when reading the play. There is more doubt when watching it for the first time. Guil starts to deliver a funeral oration, but then the Player eventually gets up to applause from the Tragedians. He has died with panache: now he is dead, now he isn't. People die somewhere else by repute. Stoppard, the retractable young blade, reveals that the Player has been acting naturally.

The Player's performance is followed by a medley of other ones from the Tragedians:

> Deaths for all ages and occasions! Deaths by suspension, convulsion, consumption, incision, execution, asphyxiation and malnutrition –! Climactic carnage, by poison and by steel –! Double deaths by duel –! Show! (p. 91)

It is carnival time as the Tragedians run riot with their dance of death. As the stage directions indicate, they perform the duel scene from *Hamlet*. The frenzied pace, together with the fact that the Shakespearian text has been reduced once again to a dumb show, means that it is transformed from tragedy into comedy.

Ros responds positively to this dumb show. Despite his professed preferences for a good clean show, he really enjoys the Player's orgies. Guil is nevertheless still plumbing his own philosophical shallows by meditating on death:

> It's the absence of presence, nothing more . . . the endless time of never coming

back . . . a gap you can't see, and when the wind blows through it, it makes no sound . . .   (pp. 91–2)

There is, however, no wind in the theatre. Like billions of other people, Ros and Guil decide to keep their appointment. Ros is the first to exit, still talking about the weather. Guil lingers a little longer trying to make head or tail of events. At least he will be better informed next time he plays the part. He then exits: 'Now you see me, now you –' (p. 92). These last words underline the point that the play as a whole has been based around childhood games and teases. Ros and Guil have just enough time to compare notes about audience reactions to their performances before they join the rest of the cast for the curtain call.

Rosencrantz finishes, as it began, in the middle of a piece of action. The lights go up to reveal that the stage is set for the final moments from *Hamlet*. Stoppard follows his practice of only allowing the audience to peep at Shakespeare's play. One of the English Ambassadors delivers the news 'that Rosencrantz and Guildenstern are dead' (p. 93). A character who has not been seen before responds to this news: 'He never gave commandment for their death' (p. 93). It is reasonably clear that Shakespeare's Horatio is telling the Ambassadors that Claudius did not sign Rosencrantz and Guildenstern's death warrant. His speech, set within the framework of Stoppard's play, is more ambiguous. It appears as if it tells a lie to protect the memory of Hamlet. Horatio, whose speech has significantly been rendered as prose, goes on to tell the Ambassadors the gist of what has happened. Stoppard cuts him short and ends the play. Fortinbras, another new character who has confusingly only appeared at the end of Stoppard's play, is not given the opportunity to deliver his funeral oration to the sound of a 'peal of ordnance'. The sombre mood at the end of *Hamlet* is undermined by Stoppard's shortened, prosaic and confusing version of it. It is also very difficult to take a stage strewn with corpses very seriously after the Tragedians' dance of death.

Part Two. The Theatre of Politics in *Hamlet*

4. The Theatre of Politics in *Hamlet*

Laying the ghost

Rosencrantz ends in the middle of Horatio's catalogue of bloody deeds rather than with Fortinbras's funeral oration. Hamlet is not lifted out from the heap of dead bodies and ceremoniously born aloft by four captains to the sound of a dead march and a volley of shots. Shakespeare's ending, itself a truncated one in that it only shows the preparations for Hamlet's funeral, is broken and its rites are maimed. *Rosencrantz* is, however, only accentuating a process which is taking place throughout *Hamlet*. As noticed, the first words indicate that a military ritual has been inverted. Here and elsewhere, the rottenness of the Danish court corrupts its rites and rituals.

Rosencrantz's juxtapositions between Shakespearian and colloquial languages also accentuate something which is present in *Hamlet*. Courtly language is shown to be empty and hollow because of breaks between the form and meaning of particular ceremonies. The most obvious illustration of this occurs just before the fencing match when Hamlet deflates through parody the courtly hyperbole of Osrick. He either questions or mimics the language used by Claudius, Polonius and their supporters throughout the play. The seeds of Stoppard's parody are contained within Shakespeare's own text. Similarly, while it is undoubtedly true that Stoppard plays some dazzling theatrical games within the framework of *Hamlet*, his representation of theatricality is at least based upon the games which Shakespeare himself plays.

Three of the distinctive features of Stoppard's re-presentation of *Hamlet* are the ways in which he maims its rites, makes its ceremonial language appear to be ridiculous and plays theatrical games with it. These are also distinctive features of Shakespeare's play. Perhaps there are other aspects of *Rosencrantz* which are not borrowed quite so directly from Shakespeare. Another list might include interrogation, doubt and irony. These are also the chapter headings which Levin uses for his study of *Hamlet*. Stoppard dramatizes in *Rosencrantz* the fact that Shakespeare in general and *Hamlet* in particular are very hard acts to follow. Every playwright probably needs to lay the ghost of *Hamlet*, although putting it this way suggests the enormity of the task. Stoppard makes a comedy out of the tragedy that Shakespeare had said almost everything before him.

Shakespeare links broken ceremony, linguistic disorder and heightened theatricality to the political climate of the Renaissance court. *Hamlet* is a claustrophobically political play which holds a mirror up to power and corruption and the ways in which they represent themselves. Stoppard only retains a limited amount of this concentration on politics. He shows that attendant lords were an expendable commodity and, by turning *Hamlet* upside down, suggests their bewilderment at the comings and goings of more powerful courtiers. Yet, as indicated, he is really concerned to play down *Hamlet*'s political themes by letting his attendant lords stand outside the web of political intrigue and corruption.

It is notoriously difficult to say 'what happens in *Hamlet*'. Stoppard exploits this problem for its comic potential in *Rosencrantz*. The following analysis of *Hamlet* seeks to establish two main points. First of all, it will provide more evidence to support the argument that Stoppard's parody of *Hamlet* has its origins within the play itself. Secondly, it will try to establish the point that Shakespeare's representation of theatricality, unlike Stoppard's, is explicitly related to his treatment of politics. Both these points have an important bearing on the argument, frequently advanced by Stoppard critics, that *Rosencrantz* defamiliarizes *Hamlet*.

Revenge

Stoppard uses Shakespeare's play as the basis of his own one. Shakespeare in his turn almost certainly used an earlier play about Hamlet as his starting point. Although the text of this play has not survived, its existence is recorded by a number of relatively reliable witnesses. It was probably written sometime in the 1580s, if not by Thomas Kyd himself then by one of his many imitators. The first performances of Shakespeare's *Hamlet* took place in 1601. The assumption has usually been that the earlier play offered a much cruder treatment of revenge. It probably had similarities with Kyd's *The Spanish Tragedy* (*c*.1588), but lacked its theatrical power and popularity. This accounts for its failure to survive. Stoppard represents Shakespeare's play as being an old-fashioned one. Shakespeare in his turn probably represented the earlier version of the Hamlet story as an old-fashioned one.

The revenge theme is part of *Hamlet*'s exploration of politics. Throughout the sixteenth century religious and political propaganda attempted to outlaw private acts of revenge. The individual who spilt blood to revenge his or her blood relatives was held to be usurping the power of higher spiritual and temporal authorities. The message was very clear, although there is inevitably more uncertainty about how it was received. The popularity of revenge dramas can be used to question the effectiveness of this propaganda. The argument is a complicated one since, at first sight, the majority of revenge plays seem to carry the same message as did Tudor propaganda: that a private act of revenge is an evil and irrational one, which damages the individual concerned as well as the body politic. This may, however, be how the conflict between the private and the public is finally resolved, but the meanings of texts do not necessarily just lie in their resolutions. Revenge dramas dramatize a conflict, which means that they were open to conflicting interpretations. The cops usually catch the robbers in our own contemporary morality plays, but that does not necessarily mean that the spectators must be on their side. Stoppard underplays *Hamlet*'s political themes by ignoring this debate about the ethics of revenge. When it is taken away, Hamlet's actions become rather meaningless, which is of course the intention.

It is still occasionally suggested that Hamlet is unsure of the morality of revenge from the very start of the play and that this prevents him from acting decisively. This misses the point that the Ghost, who urges Hamlet to revenge his death, is a problematic figure. He certainly appears to be the ghost of Hamlet's father, but he may just be acting this part to tempt Hamlet. There is no quick answer to the question of whether the Ghost is a 'spirit of health or goblin damned' (I.4.49). His credibility has to be tested before his words can be considered as commands to revenge. The question that Hamlet faces at the beginning of the play is whether it is the Ghost or Claudius who has assumed 'a pleasing shape' (II.2.598). If the Ghost is telling the truth, then Claudius is certainly revealed to be an actor who 'may smile, and smile, and be a villain' (I.5.108). Stoppard does not consider the revenge theme and therefore pays no attention to the Ghost. This brings Shakespeare's play down to earth by depriving it of its supernatural elements. It also represents a secularization of the play since the appearance of the Ghost provides the occasion for a discussion of religious attitudes towards the supernatural. The fact that the Ghost may be an actor provides an example of how Shakespeare's representation of theatricality is not divorced from the play's political themes.

Plays within plays

The Danish court is shown to be a stage on which a series of plays are being performed before the actors arrive there. If Claudius is the villain, then he plays the part of a conscientious monarch in the council chamber scene. He sends ambassadors to Norway and takes an apparently judicious interest in the welfare of both Hamlet and Laertes. Hamlet implies that Claudius may not be all he seems to be with the more general accusation that the court is based on theatrical show. He defends his decision to continue to wear mourning for his father:

> These indeed 'seem';
> For they are actions that a man might play.
> But I have that within which passes show –
> These but the trappings and the suits of woe. (I.2.83–6)

His criticism of the court is that appearances, denoted by the costumes that are worn for particular parts, have become divorced from inner convictions. There is a gap between the inner self and fashion, or fashioning. He also draws attention to the way in which the ceremonies of mourning for his father have been broken. Behind this lies the more important charge that Gertrude has broken her original marriage vows by agreeing to a hasty second marriage. One of the ironies about this speech as a whole is that Hamlet's own riddling, punning language seems to mean a number of different things. His clothes may be black but his language is brightly coloured or, in the terms of the play itself, painted. As will become more apparent, he is both the scourge of theatrical show and an accomplished practitioner of it.

Hamlet puts on a theatrical show or 'antic disposition' (I.5.172) partly to disguise his secret about the Ghost. A theatrical mask is also essential on this political stage where everybody else seems to be wearing one as well. The Ghost looks like that of his father, but this may be an illusion. Claudius plays the part of a wise ruler, although he may be a murderer. Gertrude has a regal appearance but may, according to Hamlet, be consumed by lust. Hamlet himself, particularly in his exchanges with Polonius, plays the court fool. He alters his costume and plays another part for Ophelia's benefit, namely that of a frenzied melancholic. As noted, this is how Hamlet makes his first appearance in *Rosencrantz*. The question of his 'antic disposition' is tossed around to pass the time, but the specifically political explanations for it tend to be withheld.

Hamlet is refused permission to leave the court as Claudius wants to have him watched. This task falls to Polonius, who is very much the eyes and ears of the court. He may assume the shape of a doddering old fool, although this may only be to disguise his sinister and menacing duties.

His advice to his son, Laertes, on how he ought to play his part is stuffed with platitudes about the meaning of life. Polonius plays a concerned but rather tedious father, although the extraordinarily secular nature of his advice sounds a muffled warning about his credibility as a wise counsellor. The speech is revealed to be a public performance when Polonius instructs Reynaldo to spy upon Laertes. More specifically, Reynaldo is commissioned to perform a theatrical show to test Laertes. Like almost everyone else in the play, he will use 'indirections' to 'find directions out' (II.1.66). Disguise and 'falsehood' are the 'bait' which is used to try to catch the 'truth' (II.1.63).

Polonius not only spies upon his son, but is also quite prepared to use his daughter, Ophelia, as part of a show designed to penetrate Hamlet's own shows. He outlines the scenario for this particular play to Claudius in terms which, for an Elizabethan audience, would have left no doubt that he proposes to use Ophelia like a prostitute:

> At such a time I'll loose my daughter to him.
> Be you and I behind an arras then.
> Mark the encounter. If he love her not,
> And be not from his reason fallen thereon,
> Let me be no assistant for a state,
> But keep a farm and carters. (II.2.162–7)

Such is the nature of the Danish court that, ironically, this plan to eavesdrop on a particular conversation is itself probably overheard by Hamlet. His subsequent hostility to Ophelia can be explained by the fact that he either knows, or at least suspects, that she is being used as a pawn in this political chess game. By agreeing to play this part, she betrays her friendship with Hamlet. Shakespeare's Rosencrantz and Guildenstern may also be related to the way in which a show is staged in order to find out 'directions' and 'truth'. Claudius tells them to use a roundabout route, 'draw him on to pleasures' (II.2.15), in the hope that Hamlet might, in an unguarded moment, reveal what displeases him about the Danish court. They are therefore being asked to continue to assume the pleasing shapes of friends, when they are in reality enemies. Hamlet's hostility towards them is, in very general terms, similar to his contempt for Ophelia. They betray the friendship of 'young days' (II.2.11). Stoppard makes his attendant lords the upholders of childhood, whereas Shakespeare indicates that they are the destroyers of it. Hamlet's rejection of Ophelia and Rosencrantz and Guildenstern may be explicable in terms of the fact that he sees their performances as performances.

The important question that Stoppard poses is whether the attendant lords had any choice but to go along with Claudius's theatrical show. Their rejection of Hamlet may be explicable in terms of the power politics of the Renaissance court. Similarly, Ophelia's conduct can be explained by the more specifically sexual politics of such a court. Polonius can count on her to play her part in his play to trap Hamlet because daughters were expected to offer their fathers silent obedience.

There are, then, a number of plays either already in performance, or else being plotted, before the players arrive at Elsinore. One of the myths about Hamlet, to which Stoppard subscribes, is that he is unable to make up his mind. This leads to the suggestion that the action of the play itself is slow and often painfully delayed. One of the ways in which *Rosencrantz* seeks to parody *Hamlet* is to take forms of inactivity and indecision to comic extremes. Alternatively, Hamlet can be seen as a very quick-witted, fast-talking improviser. He has the ability to effect a number of quick changes: playing the court fool for Polonius, the melancholic lover for Ophelia and the ambitious young man for Rosencrantz and Guildenstern. Speed is the name of the game as he has to make sure that he is always at least one theatrical jump ahead of Claudius. This suggests that the pace of the play, far from being tortuous, might be close to that associated with political thrillers. Shakespeare's *Hamlet*, unlike Stoppard's version of it, is concerned with the defence and inheritance of the realm. The question of Hamlet's indecision will be considered again in relation to the events surrounding the disruption of *The Murder of Gonzago*. It would be dangerous to leave the impression, however, that interpretations of Hamlet the delayer and Hamlet the improviser are irreconcilable ones. It can be argued, for instance, that improvisation becomes for Hamlet an end in itself rather than a means to an end.

The arrival of the Players provides a good example of the speed with which Hamlet is able to improvise upon events. It is quite difficult to establish when he decides to use them as part of his plot against Claudius. His welcome initially takes the form of theatrical pleasantries, which include a reference to the fact that the actor who plays the female parts may be getting too old for the part. Shakespeare provides a quick sketch for Stoppard's Alfred. The plan probably starts forming in Hamlet's mind very early on, since his choice of a part for the First Player to perform is not a random one. With Hamlet himself alternating between the parts of actor, spectator and director, the First Player delivers a long speech about how Pyrrhus avenged the death of his father, Achilles, by killing Priam. Pyrrhus has moments of delay which heighten the dramatic tension of the speech, but is represented as being a revenger who does not equivocate over ethical questions. Hamlet watches a performance of the part which the Ghost wants him to play. Adding the parts of both impresario and author to his repertoire, he commissions a performance of *The Murder of Gonzago* and insists that it should include 'a speech of some dozen lines or sixteen lines, which I would set down and insert in't' (II.2.538–9). As noticed, Stoppard suggests that performers and patrons are interchangeable parts. This idea is taken from *Hamlet* rather than brought to it. Hamlet certainly alternates between a number of parts in this scene, although it should also be noted that Polonius, Rosencrantz, Guildenstern and possibly the other Players act the parts of spectators during it. Polonius in particular provides a very self-conscious, and self-important, on-stage audience. The practice of showing an audience a reflection of itself on stage does not originate with Shakespeare, although *Hamlet* remains one of the most complex exercises in it. The speech which Hamlet inserts into *The Murder of Gonzago* represents the precise manner in which the Ghost described his own death. Claudius's response to it will therefore confirm or deny his guilt. It is often difficult to keep up with both the speed and ingenuity of Hamlet's improvisations.

There are at this moment in the play two main theatrical shows in preparation: Claudius and Polonius are planning to use Ophelia as a decoy, while Hamlet prepares to counter-attack by using the Players as his decoy. Claudius and Polonius strike first. Ophelia is directed to remain on stage, and they take up their positions as a concealed audience. Claudius outlines the plot to Gertrude:

> Her father and myself, lawful espials,
> We'll so bestow ourselves that, seeing unseen,
> We may of their encounter frankly judge,
> And gather by him, as he is behaved,
> If't be th'affliction of his love or no
> That thus he suffers for.   (III.1.32–7)

The political atmosphere of the Danish court is such that the use of indirections and concealment can be passed off as quite legitimate. The script calls for Ophelia to hand back to Hamlet some love tokens that he has given to her. Lisa Jardine argues that Hamlet and Ophelia are already betrothed, although later textual references to their relationship cast some doubt on this reading. She nevertheless emphasizes the important point about this scene by showing that it is a betrothal in reverse, or an anti-ceremony. Ophelia returns gifts instead of receiving them and members of both families are either absentees or spectators rather than participants. Although betrothal was essentially a family or social ceremony, it nevertheless carried important religious associations and consequences. Ophelia is being asked to act out a religious part in this scene. She is directed to assume an attitude of religious devotion and to wait for Hamlet to accost her. The fact that she is honouring her father by playing this scene at all suggests that her devotion is genuine. As far as Claudius and Polonius are concerned, however, religious piety is just another part to be played in their theatre of politics. This provides part of the reason why the Danish court can only stage either broken ceremonies or else ones which invert and subvert traditional practices.

Claudius and Polonius's plot is unsuccessful because Hamlet either knows or suspects what is happening. The nunnery scene therefore becomes a game of bluff, double bluff. If Hamlet can convince the on-stage spectators that he is primarily concerned with affairs of the heart, then they might not suspect that he is also interested in affairs of state. Polonius treats Ophelia like a prostitute and then so does Hamlet. It is not adequate to claim that he is merely playing a part when he humiliates her. He believes that she has betrayed their friendship. He is also, at a more general level, profoundly disturbed by female sexuality. His responses to it are extreme and stereotypical ones: women are either to be worshipped as saints, or else they are to be treated contemptuously as prostitutes. Ophelia is made to play the part of a saint for this scene. Hamlet makes her play, and needs to make her play, the part of a prostitute. His hysterical responses to women will be considered again during the discussion of the closet scene. *Rosencrantz* contains a fragment from the nunnery scene, but virtually ignores *Hamlet*'s complicated and disturbing representation of sexual politics. Ros and Guil are allowed to cultivate their particular brand of male friendship, which possibly parallels Hamlet's relationship with Horatio, in splendid isolation from women. Stoppard turns *Hamlet* upside down and in doing so manages to pour away its political themes.

Audience reactions to Hamlet's performance during the nunnery scene are divided ones. Polonius believes that his interpretation of 'neglected love' (III.1.179) is confirmed and prepares for another act in this particular drama, which will star Gertrude rather than Ophelia. Claudius is not convinced that Hamlet is merely concerned with affairs of the heart and so improvises the scenario to send him to England. Hamlet admits later on to Horatio that Claudius's plot, implemented by Rosencrantz and Guildenstern, catches him unawares:

> Being thus be-netted round with villainies,
> Or I could make a prologue to my brains
> They had begun the play.   (V.2.29–31)

As suggested, the movement of *Hamlet* needs to be seen in terms of a series of plays within plays. The speed with which they are both improvised and performed means that the theatre audience, like Hamlet, may find it difficult to establish when one has finished and another one started.

The Murder of Gonzago

Hamlet's advice to the Players offers a commentary on the contemporary 'war of the theatres'. When it is set within the more specific context of the play itself, it provides a warning to the Players not to overact. Hamlet believes that what might be described as a direct acting style will only alert Claudius to the fact that the counter-attack has already begun. He therefore tries to make sure that the Players use a more indirect, or subtle, approach. This is the bait which will eventually net the big fish. He and Horatio will play their parts as spectators in an equally subtle way. They will appear, or seem, to watch the play, while they are in fact watching Claudius:

> I prithee, when thou seest that act afoot,
> Even with the very comment of thy soul
> Observe my uncle. If his occulted guilt
> Do not itself unkennel in one speech,
> It is a damnèd ghost that we have seen,
> And my imaginations are as foul
> As Vulcan's stithy. Give him heedful note.
> For I mine eyes will rivet to his face,
> And after we will both our judgements join
> In censure of his seeming.   (III.2.88–97)

A theatrical show is to be used to find out whether it is Claudius or the Ghost who has assumed a pleasing, theatrical shape in order to disguise their true directions.

Hamlet's advice to the Players goes largely unheeded. Their production of *The Murder of Gonzago* retains many of the old-fashioned techniques and conventions which he had criticized. Part of the visual comedy in *Rosencrantz* comes from a clash between the mannered, old-fashioned acting associated with the court scenes and the more modern, fluid style of Ros and Guil. Once again, this is something which is taken from *Hamlet* rather than brought to it. The Players choose to introduce their play with a dumb show, despite the fact that Hamlet had implied that such forms of entertainment were not appropriate for a sophisticated court audience. Although dumb shows were a common enough feature of Elizabethan plays, Shakespeare himself tended to use them sparingly as a comic device to bring styles of acting into conflict. This is one of the functions of the Mechanicals' dumb show in *A Midsummer Night's Dream.*

The dumb show which precedes *The Murder of Gonzago* offers a direct and explicit representation of Claudius's crimes. It should therefore, in theory, warn him that the counter-attack has already begun. The prologue leaves no doubt that Hamlet's improvised play, itself a play within a play within a play, has already begun. The question of whether Claudius pays any attention to the dumb show is one of the more difficult textual riddles. He *seems* to ignore it, but this does not necessarily mean that he does so.

Leaving aside some of the more controversial points about the precise layout of the Elizabethan theatre, it is reasonably clear that the Players are meant to perform at the rear of the stage. The on-stage spectators should probably take up their positions on either side of this playing area. Claudius, Polonius and Gertrude position themselves on one side, while Hamlet, Ophelia and Horatio group themselves together on the other one. Such patterning allows the theatre spectators to link themselves with the on-stage ones, while at the same time placing the 'mighty opposites' opposite each other. The court processes on in an imposing manner for the performance to the sound of trumpets and kettledrums. The entrance of the spectators is itself a performance. They provide the spectacle. As indicated, Hamlet and Horatio will spend as much time watching Claudius as they will watching the play. At a more general level, it ought to be assumed that attendant lords and guards pay almost as much attention to the spectacle of King Claudius watching a play as they do to the play itself. Shakespeare spins an actor–spectator coin, although his one is part of the political currency of the Renaissance court.

Hamlet continues to improvise and alternate his parts. Besides acting a spectator, he plays the parts of patron and stage-manager. These are all mixed in with the continuation of the role based around 'antic disposition'. *The Murder of Gonzago* opens with Gonzago trying to persuade Baptista that she ought to marry again if he dies. Their speeches are almost entirely in rhymed couplets, which means that they have to be delivered in a stiff, formal manner. They are also long-winded ones. Gertrude's comment that 'The lady doth protest too much, methinks' (III.2.240) represents a theatrical criticism or review, as well as a moral judgement. Here and elsewhere, the theatre audience is shown an on-stage one reviewing a production which is still in performance. Alvin Kernan shows how the themes of this production heighten the theatricality of this part of *Hamlet*. He describes the Player King as 'an actor in a play playing an actor king talking about life as a series of changing roles'. This might apply to Claudius as well, except that he takes care not to draw attention to the fact that he is role playing.

Gonzago goes to sleep in his garden. His nephew, Lucianus, enters to poison him. Hamlet provides a running commentary on the theatrical events. He is the author of this part of the play as well as a spectator of it. He also acts as a chorus to it. John Dover Wilson's interpretation of this part of *Hamlet* tends to be too schematic, although he is probably right to insist that Hamlet is concerned that direct or overacting will give the game away too early. Hamlet plays the part of prompter to try to stop the actor playing Lucianus from overplaying:

. . . Begin, murderer. Pox, leave thy damnable faces and begin. Come; the croaking raven doth bellow for revenge   (III.2.261–3)

Hamlet prompts an actor but, at another level, he also prompts himself. Like Lucianus, he is the nephew of a king whom he may have to kill out of revenge. Lucianus spends time self-consciously acting the part of a revenger and appears unwilling to carry out the act of revenge itself. This is precisely the discrepancy between acting and action which Hamlet agonized over in the earlier 'O, what a rogue and peasant slave am I!' soliloquy (II.2.547–603). Although he certainly criticizes himself for his delay in taking action in this soliloquy, it is worth emphasizing the point that he concludes it by stating, quite reasonably, that it is essential to test the Ghost's credibility before thinking about revenge. Lucianus, the seemingly reluctant revenger, may be taken as a representation of Hamlet as he is. It probably makes more sense, however, to see him as a representation of what Hamlet might become.

Hamlet believes that Claudius's exit from the play, which provides another example of broken ceremony, confirms that the Ghost was telling the truth. Claudius is shown two related things. First of all, that Hamlet knows his guilty secret and, secondly, that his nephew intends to revenge the crime. *The Murder of Gonzago* therefore comments on the past and warns about the future. It offers representations of Claudius, Gertrude and Hamlet himself, all of whom are also self-conscious members of an on-stage audience. As spectators, they either comment on or ask for explanations of the play which represents them. Hamlet, in particular, plays a bewildering number of roles. Besides being both an actor and a spectator, he is also an impresario, an author, a reviewer, a stage-manager and a prompter. The direct acting and formal speaking of the Players contrasts with the subtlety with which both Claudius and Hamlet play their different parts in Shakespeare's theatre of politics. The performance holds a mirror up to the theatre as well as providing another occasion which reflects the nature of the political power game. Claudius's theatrical show is exposed for what it is by the theatrical show which Hamlet improvises out of the chance appearance of the Players at Elsinore.

Broken ceremonies

The disruption of the play does not disrupt Claudius and Polonius's plot to stage a scene between Hamlet and Gertrude. The fact that Hamlet willingly agrees to play this scene, conscious that it almost certainly is a scene stage-managed by his enemies, is another of the play's more complicated puzzles. If the argument about the need to test the Ghost's credibility is accepted, then this is really the first moment when Hamlet can be accused of delay. Possible explanations for his decision, which represents a form of indecision, might include the following ones. He has proved, or seems to have proved, Claudius's guilt but does not know whether Gertrude was an accomplice. It therefore makes sense to try to discover the full extent of guilt before taking revenge. A more convincing explanation is that Hamlet appears, or seems, to be concerned with Claudius's guilt, whereas within himself he is much more concerned with what he takes to be Gertrude's crime. It is not particularly relevant to establish whether or not she was involved with the murder, since the crime that Hamlet has in mind is the one of being a woman. To put the point more precisely, her crime is that she refuses to conform to Hamlet's ideal, or saintly, woman. Although this explanation fits in with what takes place in the closet scene itself, there is another one which offers a reading based more on theatricality than psychology. Hamlet, the great improviser, is unable to resist the chance to perform in this, or in any other, scene. It is at this point in the play that acting is revealed to be an end in itself rather than a means to an end.

There is a sense in which these explanations are irrelevant since Hamlet has the chance to kill Claudius before he reaches his mother's closet. Claudius is, however, praying for forgiveness, so Hamlet decides to postpone the act of revenge. His argument, or perhaps excuse, is that to kill somebody while they are praying would only ensure that their soul went straight to heaven. As Alan Dessen points out, Hamlet is quite happy to accept an appearance as the reality. Despite his awareness of the ways in which the Danish court is founded on seemings and shows, he believes what he sees in his role as a spectator. Claudius nevertheless reveals to the theatre audience that his attempt to pray has been an unsuccessful one. This makes his act of praying another of the play's broken rituals in the sense that it is incomplete and unsuccessful. It is, however, ironic that it is one of the few rituals which is not broken in the sense of being interrupted. The villain is given a chance to say his prayers. Claudius is alone, insofar as anybody is alone at this claustrophobic court, so there is no reason to suspect that he is staging what turns out to be a show of repentance for anybody's benefit but his own. The theatrical nature of the court, however, means that such a suspicion cannot be entirely discounted. Claudius has already proved in the staging of the meeting between Hamlet and Ophelia that he is quite prepared to use religion as a front, or decoy.

Polonius adds the finishing touches to his script. He urges Gertrude to speak sternly to Hamlet and then takes up his familiar position as a concealed, on-stage spectator. Hamlet's part in the closet scene is a continuation of the one he played in the council chamber. He holds a mirror up to Gertrude in order to reveal her artificiality and theatricality. His part is also a continuation of the one he played in the nunnery scene in which he accuses Ophelia of being a painted lady. The use of paint, or make-up, denotes theatricality but it also signifies that a woman is a prostitute. Claudius, for instance, makes this connection in a revealing aside just before the nunnery scene:

> The harlot's cheek, beautied with plastering art,
> Is not more ugly to the thing that helps it
> Than is my deed to my most painted word.   (III.1.51–3)

References to painting, colouring, gilding and sugaring run throughout the play. As Claudius's comment indicates, language as well as ceremonies are based upon deceit. There is, however, an important contradiction at the heart of Hamlet's attempt to get Gertrude to face up to what he takes to be her deceitful nature. As pointed out earlier on, he is both the scourge of courtly seemings and an accomplished exponent of them. He gives a very theatrical performance against theatricality, complete with self-conscious gestures such as the use of the mirror and the portraits of Gertrude's two husbands. There is another way of drawing attention to this fundamental contradiction. Hamlet wants Gertrude to see herself as she really is, yet this is precisely what he is unable to do himself. He gives a performance based on his revulsion at the fact that Gertrude has transgressed against his idealized conception of women. Yet his dramatic recreation of the intimate details of her relationship with Claudius suggests that he is attracted by what he gives the appearance of finding repellent. He continues to linger on, or paw over, these details despite the fact that he has just murdered Polonius. As Dessen argues, his casual response to Polonius's death can be interpreted in terms of 'not seeing' what he has done. He tries to open Gertrude's eyes, but his own are closed to the reality of both his actions and his desires. His attack on theatricality takes the form of a performance structured around seemings and appearances. His words are as 'painted' as those of Claudius.

Hamlet stops to speak with a Captain when he is being escorted by Rosencrantz and Guildenstern to the boat for England. This soldier tells him about Fortinbras's military exploits but sets them in an unheroic context:

> Truly to speak, and with no addition,
> We go to gain a little patch of ground
> That hath in it no profit but the name. (IV.4.17–19)

Such 'addition' is an essential part of the process of making things seem to be what they are not in the theatres of politics and war. By the 'addition' of a ceremonial language, Fortinbras can transform a meaningless military exercise into a heroic quest. By the 'addition' of a smile or the clichés about divine right which are delivered to Laertes, Claudius is able to play the part of a king. The Captain suggests that the ceremonial language of the court is broken in the sense that there is an unbridgeable gap between appearance and reality. Hamlet, the courtier as well as the scourge of courtiers, is not prepared to accept this conclusion. His admiration for warlords like his own father or Fortinbras allows him to retain a belief in honour:

> Rightly to be great
> Is not to stir without great argument,
> But greatly to find quarrel in a straw
> When honour's at the stake. (IV.4.53–6)

Hamlet has always been conscious of the ways in which courtly language is based on 'addition' or 'painting', although his own continues to exhibit these characteristics until the graveyard scene.

Ophelia's language breaks free from courtly additions before Hamlet's begins to do so. Her mode of address earlier on in the play is a correct and deferential one. Her constant repetition of the phrase 'my lord', or its equivalents, to both Polonius and Hamlet draws attention to her passive obedience. She also perhaps defers to them in the sense that, as is revealed during her madness, her courtly language is not her own but a copy of theirs. This is part of a more general pattern. Gertrude becomes Claudius's echo at times in public. Ophelia rejects courtly language in her madness and cultivates instead more popular idioms. Her version of pastoralism reconnects her to childhood, or at least to a more unrepressed world, as well as to nature. It therefore draws attention to the ways in which courtly ceremonies have broken their connections with these particular worlds. The court's ceremonies are broken ones because they have lost touch with festivity.

Polonius was buried without the traditional ceremonies and Ophelia's funeral continues this pattern of 'maimèd rites'. Her position at court guarantees that, despite her suicide, she is given a funeral, although it does not contain the usual prayers and sung requiem for the dead. It seems like a funeral and yet it is not one. It is also cruelly ironic that Ophelia, the victim of the courtly power game, is only given this appearance of a funeral because of the court's influence over the church. Hamlet and Horatio are already at the graveyard when the funeral procession arrives there. They have been reflecting upon the inability of various kinds of 'addition' to withstand the fact of death. Politicians, courtiers, lawyers and landowners may cover up their intentions with elaborate phrases, but this will not prevent all of them from being covered up by a gravedigger. The recognition of this inescapable fact means that the Gravedigger himself takes a very literal, down to earth attitude to language. Hamlet realizes that to talk to him about death, and therefore about life, everything has to be spoken 'by the card' (V.1.136). There is no room for either 'equivocation' (V.1.135–6) or refinement. The punning, jesting language of the court fool did not prevent Yorick from becoming one of the dour Gravedigger's clients. Incidentally, the fact that Elsinore does not have a resident fool anymore, apart from the occasions when Hamlet plays the part, may be related to the previous point about the way in which ceremony has become divorced from festivity. Painted ladies and conquering heroes will also find that their literal and metaphorical additions are stripped away by death.

Laertes, now in league with the scheming Claudius, performs the part of a grieving brother at Ophelia's grave. His speech is self-consciously theatrical and he accompanies it with the dramatic gesture of jumping into the grave. Hamlet tries to call this theatrical bluff:

> What is he whose grief
> Bears such an emphasis, whose phrase of sorrow
> Conjures the wandering stars, and makes them stand
> Like wonder-wounded hearers? This is I,
> Hamlet the Dane.   (V.1.250–54)

He once again draws attention to the ways in which courtly language, and actions, depend on 'emphasis' or 'addition'. Here and later on he mimics Laertes's style of delivery and probably the gestures that go with it as well. His critique of theatricality, depending as it does here on the acting out of a parody, is also a celebration of it.

Hamlet is living on borrowed time since his return to Denmark. He is nevertheless quite content to pass this time by playing theatrical games. His parody of Laertes becomes an end in itself as it does not reveal the specific nature of the plot that Claudius is improvising around Laertes's return. Similarly, his parody of Osrick is another of his highly theatrical critiques of theatricality. Osrick personifies, and also caricatures, a court which is based on 'addition' and 'emphasis'. His attempts to play the courtier are both comic and menacing, as are Rosencrantz and Guildenstern's equally clumsy ones. Like them, he affects a breeding and a breed of courtesy which he does not possess. His exaggerated, or emphatic, flourishes with his hat mock the very ceremonies of greeting which he is trying to perform. He overacts the part. His gestures and clothes are borrowed ones. His language, no more than a series of flourishes which covers up its emptiness through 'addition' and repetition, is also revealed to be a borrowed costume. He overacts a part that he has under-rehearsed and is therefore an easy target for Hamlet's theatrical parody. The problem is that, as a hollow man, Osrick does not represent a conventional target. He remains oblivious to Hamlet's parody, or at least seems to do so. This particular game is therefore bound to represent a dead end.

Osrick self-importantly bears a message from Claudius which invites Hamlet to take part in a fencing match with Laertes. The messenger, himself no more than a commodity, lists the various commodities or items which form part of Claudius's ostentatious wager:

The King, sir, hath wagered with him six Barbary horses, against the which he

has impawned, as I take it, six French rapiers and poniards, with their assigns as
girdle, hangers, and so.   (V.2.145–8)

Jacques Lacan describes these as being 'collector's items' and so draws
attention to the way in which the Danish court transmutes heroic values
into just another commodity to be acquired and ultimately to be ex-
ploited. It also exploits people as possessions. Polonius owns Ophelia
and uses her as the bait with which to catch Hamlet, just as Claudius
uses some of the items from his opulent collection to entice Hamlet into
taking part in the fencing match. These items may seem to represent the
grandeur and stability of the court, but they are in fact the trappings
which disguise the rottenness, and increasing hollowness, at its core.
Lacan's phrase is also useful because it emphasizes the importance of
spectacle: a collection is there to be looked at rather than to be used.
Claudius only uses these items as part of a spectacle. Their military
function has no meaning in a world in which spectacle is defined as the
only reality. Hamlet's nostalgic recreation of the world of the warlords
offers a sharp contrast to this one in which Claudius and Osrick praise
quantity rather than quality, show rather than substance.

The fencing match, like the early stages of the performance of *The
Murder of Gonzago*, gives every appearance of being a grand but festive
occasion. Members of the court process on once again to the sounds of
trumpets and drums. They arrange themselves, conscious of order and
degree, into an on-stage audience. Claudius is the master of these festive
ceremonies. He takes the stage to insist that Hamlet and Laertes should
join hands to offer a public affirmation, or performance, of their friendship. Their ritualized greeting becomes the prologue to the spectacle
for the on-stage audience, which may even applaud parts of it. This
ceremony of friendship and harmony is a broken one because of the
divorce between show and substance. Claudius, wreathed no doubt in
smiles, leads Laertes towards Hamlet. He plays the part of the wise
monarch who is anxious to restore peace and harmony to his kingdom.
He too may receive applause for playing his part. He is, in reality,
initiating what he knows will be a mortal combat. One of the rapiers,
which ought to symbolize play within the overall context of military
honour, is baited with poison. The fencing match therefore represents
the most deadly trap that has been baited for Hamlet.

The question of whether Hamlet walks into this trap with his eyes
open is another of the more difficult textual riddles. It is easy enough to
see what parts both Claudius and Laertes are playing, but Hamlet's

performance appears to be a more complicated one. He is not attracted to the fencing match by the prizes that Osrick vulgarly dangles before him. The graveyard scene has drawn attention to the irrelevance of such ostentatious items. Although he may suspect that there is a plot against him, his theatrical games have failed to reveal any precise details about it. He tells Horatio that he has reconciled himself to 'providence' (V.2.214), which means that he is prepared to allow others to take the initiative. He has, indeed, been playing parts in other people's plays since the disruption of *The Murder of Gonzago*. He is content to play the closet scene, which was stage-managed by Polonius, and one on board the ship for England, which was improvised by Claudius. He interrupts the scene which Laertes initiates during Ophelia's funeral. His acceptance of the wager for the fencing match, which is also a part in somebody else's play, therefore fits into an overall pattern. He takes part in the scene, perhaps, because he is unable to resist the temptation of playing to the courtly gallery. He may be the scourge of courtly shows, but he also wants to be a performer in them. This, rather than the more conventional explanations based on indecision, may represent his tragic flaw or, to phrase it more precisely, the contradiction which he is unable to resolve. Perhaps he is ready and waiting for the trap to be sprung, as he implies to Horatio when he claims that 'The readiness is all' (V.2.216). There is less doubt about the fact that he is ready and eagerly waiting for the opportunity to improvise a part or two on the courtly stage.

He attempted to mock the ceremonies of the court in the council chamber scene by explicitly drawing attention to their artificiality. This time he appears to mock, or break, them by playing them to the hilt. His formal speech of reconciliation to Laertes, in which he refers to himself in the third person, is entirely appropriate for this ceremonial occasion. Having said this, however, it is also true that the use of the third person allows him to establish a distance between Hamlet, the part in this scene, and Hamlet, the actor who plays it. Laertes has his suspicions that this part is being overplayed. He claims that Hamlet 'mocks' (V.2.252) him with some of his courtly wordplay. Hamlet denies this by affirming that his performance is entirely in keeping with the symbolic gestures of this formal occasion: 'No, by this hand' (V.2.252). This time he seems to parody courtly performances by giving one himself.

The potentially festive nature of this occasion is, of course, completely broken by the deaths of Gertrude, Laertes, Claudius and Hamlet himself. Claudius sees Gertrude inadvertently drinking from the poisoned chalice, but still manages to keep up his front of the smiling king while she dies.

The show has to stay on and go on. This suggests that Gertrude, like Ophelia, is just another commodity. She is merely an item that Claudius has collected to enhance the appearance of his kingship. Rebecca Smith suggests in an important revisionist study that this is a part which Gertrude is content to play even to her death. She dies without implicating Claudius.

Hamlet attempts to deliver the kind of formal dying speech which provides explanations. He is as conscious as ever of being an actor on the courtly stage:

> You that look pale and tremble at this chance,
> That are but mutes or audiences to this act,
> Had I but time – as this fell sergeant, Death,
> Is strict in his arrest – O, I could tell you –
> But let it be.   (V.2.328–32)

He is, however, no longer able to dramatize a life which has been based on self-dramatization. He has to leave Horatio to tell his 'story' (V.2.343). His dying speech is therefore another of the potentially ceremonial moments in the play which is broken or 'maimèd'.

Conclusions

This analysis set out with two main objectives. The first was to establish that Stoppard's parody has its origins within *Hamlet* itself. His representations of broken ceremony, linguistic disorder and heightened theatricality are taken from Shakespeare's play rather than brought to it for the first time. The point requires emphasis since the majority of Stoppard critics have allowed their own sketchy knowledge of *Hamlet* to influence readings of *Rosencrantz*, which play up the differences between the two plays. The second objective was to consider in some detail the nature and extent of the differences. The analysis has tried to show that *Hamlet* is a political play, both in its representation of a power struggle to the death at a court and in its related treatment of sexual politics. Politics and theatricality are not divorced, as they are in *Rosencrantz*, but shown to be closely related. The suggestion has been made that Hamlet's tragedy is that he allows theatricality to become an end in itself in a world in which it is fatal to do so. This argument obviously needs to be developed in more detail than there is room to do here. It does, nevertheless, establish the more general point that Shakespeare, unlike Stoppard, is not just celebrating theatricality. Anne Righter has argued that the very fact that the theatre becomes the chronicler of historical stories and events provides a celebration of its power and position. This is certainly true, although the stories themselves often reveal the darker side of theatricality through its associations with corruption, disguise and intrigue. Such revelations take place in the English history plays as well as in *Hamlet*. Enough has probably been said during the analysis of *Hamlet* to suggest that it explores the weaknesses as well as the strengths of theatricality, in other words that it reveals contradictions rather than just revelling in celebrations.

Stoppard critics frequently argue that *Rosencrantz* defamiliarizes *Hamlet*. There are, as indicated, important qualifications that need to be made to this interpretation. There is also a sense in which a woolly term like defamiliarizes disguises what is going on. *Rosencrantz* depoliticizes *Hamlet*. It turns Shakespeare's play upside down and empties away potentially unpleasant subjects such as political corruption and sexual manipulation. Stoppard is in fact really doing no more than many Shakespearian commentators and directors did before him. *Hamlet* has frequently been represented as being a play about a man who is unable to make up his mind. Critics like Coleridge identified and sympathized with Hamlet's problem, while others like T. S. Eliot argued that he was making too much fuss about nothing. Stoppard takes this latter position. He defamiliarizes *Hamlet* in the sense that he inverts, edits and generally plays games with it. This disguises the fact that his parody version still offers a remarkably familiar version of the themes of the play. He may not take Hamlet's personal problems seriously, but is still suggesting that this is what the play is about. Such interpretations, whether offered reverently or irreverently produce good, clean, uncontroversial productions which are capable of filling the theatres of Europe and elsewhere. Political Shakespeare invites more divided responses.

Part Three. Writing about Writing

5. Stoppard and Genre Parody

Lord Malquist and Mr Moon

The publication of Stoppard's one and only novel, *Lord Malquist and Mr Moon*, coincided with the success of *Rosencrantz* at the Edinburgh Festival in 1966. The novel lacks the plays's control although not its irreverence. Both could have been sub-titled 'nothing sacred'. They are also both concerned with the creative process itself rather than with more conventional naturalistic or realistic themes. *Rosencrantz* is about the theatre. *Malquist* concentrates on the process of writing and reading prose narratives. Stoppard's theatre of theatre may be more polished than this single attempt at metafiction, but they are both products of his artistic self-consciousness.

Malquist is indeed a stream of self-consciousness. All the characters belong to different novels, so there is a continuous clash of styles. It is rather like going to the cinema to see a particular film, only to find that there are several others fighting for possession of the screen at the same time. Stoppard, the mischievous projectionist, keeps his audience reeling by chopping and changing the reels with bewildering speed. The novel is set at the time of Winston Churchill's funeral (1965). Malquist's running commentary on the landmarks on the route of the funeral procession parodies the hushed, reverential tones associated with the BBC. The solemnity of the occasion is also mocked by the way in which it is first ignored and then disrupted by Stoppard's characters. Stoppard, on his own way to becoming a national institution, enjoys poking fun at the competition. *Rosencrantz* attempts to deflate a Shakespearian hero, while *Malquist* refuses to allow us to praise famous men and the fathers that begat us. We may have gone to the cinema to see a dignified documentary or newsreel of a sombre event, but the projectionist insists on juxtaposing it with cartoons and caricatures. Joe Orton also refused to eulogize Churchill in *What the Butler Saw* (1969). A statue of the great man is blown up in a gas explosion and bits of it impregnate the unfortunate Mrs Barclay. Orton's tone, here and elsewhere, is anarchic, whereas Stoppard's is only teasingly playful.

Stoppard's novel parodies other forms of writing, particularly popular genre fiction. Malquist's relationship with Jane Moon is straight out of the Regency romances of Georgette Heyer and Barbara Cartland. There are thus endless descriptions of clothes and furniture. Malquist, the dandy, enjoys watching his own performance in the part:

My Regency coat for gaming at the club is of a brocade as blue as the midnight sky over Firenze. My gloves are lilac, my hose is white, my cravat is of the palest blue silk, my boots are the hand-stitched hide of unborn gazelles . . .   (p. 10)

Jane, like every good Cartland heroine, passes the time by dressing, undressing and having a bath. She is a great believer in dramatic entrances:

Jane came into view at the bend of the stairs wearing a dress of peacock colours, gold-frogged round the neck and down one side as far as the slit which began at her stocking-top. She flung out her bare arms with a cry of '*Darlings!*' and stopped the movie of her descent for a few frames in order to experience it.

(p. 38)

The actress is also a spectator. The parody of the Regency romance has merged into one of the Hollywood musical. No movie is, however, allowed to dominate the screen for too long. Jane's admirers include two cowboys called Long John Slaughter and Jasper Jones. The plot is absurd, although Stoppard is not an absurdist because he always contrives to provide logical explanations for absurd events. These cowboys are making a commercial for Western-style pork and beans. Similarly, the bizarre spectacles in *After Magritte* (1970) are provided with rational explanations. The presence of the cowboys means that another movie is already on the screen, this time probably Paul Newman in *The Left-Handed Gun* (1958):

Sitting easy in the saddle, L. J. (for Long John) Slaughter moseyed down the slope, hat low over his eyes. The things you noticed were the single gun on his left hip and the tough leather chaps that covered his denims though this wasn't cactus country. Slaughter was a left-handed gun and he had the look of a man who had come a long way.   (p. 12)

Slaughter lives up to his name, as many Stoppard characters do, by staging a shoot-out with Jones during the funeral procession. Just to prove that nothing is sacred, a drunken Irishman, who believes that he is the Risen Christ, interrupts the procession as well. He believes that the crowds lining the streets have come to see him.

The parody of the funeral is intensified by the fact that the Risen Christ is sitting astride two bodies, which have been wrapped up in a carpet and placed on top of his donkey. These are the bodies of Marie, the Moons' French maid, and the General, who was in the habit of calling on her for French correction. Their relationship allows Stoppard to parody popular pornography. Lady Malquist's sexual and alcoholic cravings offer an extension of this theme, although she is also being cast as a mysterious lady from the *film noir* genre. She, like Jane, is not allowed to wallow in her own movie for too long. The projectionist keeps juxtaposing it with scenes from P. G. Wodehouse. Moon finds himself involved in the heroic mission of fetching Lady Malquist a bottle of scotch, which he can only do with the assistance of the Butler:

And flashing the old retainer one of my sunnier smiles I legged it upstairs with the water of life clutched to my bosom, and grinning like a golden retriever coming back to base with the first pheasant of the season.   (p. 133)

Moon, alias Bertie Wooster, is an unlikely bedfellow for the mysterious Lady Malquist. P. G. Wodehouse and Raymond Chandler may have gone to the same school, but belong to different stylistic schools.

Malquist is metafictional in the general sense because it is stuffed with parodies. It is also metafictional in a more specific sense because both the main characters are writers. Malquist writes but probably does not send letters to *The Times*. He is also preparing a monograph on book titles which are derived from quotations from *Hamlet*. He has not yet reached 'Rosencrantz and Guildenstern are dead'. *Malquist*, itself no more than a series of incomplete sketches, is littered with unfinished, perhaps unfinishable, manuscripts. Whereas Malquist works on his monograph at a gentlemanly pace, Moon is unable to get beyond the first sentence of his history of the world. He gathers and organizes his material but the act of writing defeats him. He therefore hires himself out as a latter-day Boswell to earn some quick money. He is hired by Malquist, who wishes his *pensées* to be immortalized. Remarks such as 'to drink creme de menthe in a pale blue cravat would be the abandonment of everything I stand for' (p. 62) do not deserve to be casually abandoned. Like the Risen Christ, Moon sets himself up in the 'posterity' (p. 56) business. Writing about writing and writers is one of Stoppard's major themes. George Moore dictates a philosophical lecture throughout *Jumpers* (1972). As will be shown later on, *Travesties* (1974) concentrates on writers, and would-be writers, who lived in Zurich during the First World War. *Dirty Linen* (1976) is about the activities of a Select Committee which is preparing a report on 'Promiscuity in High Places'. It also focuses on popular journalism, which is explored again in *Professional Foul* (1977) through the two sports journalists, Grayson and Chamberlain. The philosophers in this television play are all writers of articles, lectures or theses. The conflict between two foreign correspondents, Wagner and Milne, is at the centre of *Night and Day* (1978). *The Real Thing* (1982) concerns the conflict between two playwrights. Henry is a successful writer of polished, West End plays, while Brodie believes that the theatre needs political agitprop.

Moon the biographer ought to be a spectator who chronicles the wit and wisdom of his great patron. Stoppard flips the actor–spectator coin again by making Malquist affect to be a spectator as well. Malquist argues that the heroic age associated with men of action such as Churchill must give way to one in which the spectator is the only hero. His stylishly aloof manner indicates that he is just such a modern hero. The point is made ironically for Malquist, far from being modern, exists in a world which does not recognize the existence of the twentieth century. His dandified appearance is enhanced by the carriage in which he bowls around London, bowling over anybody who gets in his way. He owns a pet lion and a falcon, which wreak their own kind of havoc on the modern metropolis. As a spectator, Malquist watches modern times from the privileged distance of a past aristocracy. Moon therefore has the job being a spectator of a spectator. He starts writing his journal in the measured tones of James Boswell himself. The uneventful content nevertheless undermines this grand tone. His daily trips to the library to research his unwritable book on world history are hardly epic journeys or quests. Like Ros and Guil, he is fascinated by the weather.

Moon's trivial pursuits look as if they might come to an end with the arrival of Malquist on the scene. The problem here is that all Moon's notes of their first meeting have been burnt. Stoppard exposes the chaos that reigns while Moon, and perhaps every writer, composes a composed narrative. He did this again in *Jumpers* in which George Moore attempts to compose his lecture in the midst of a murder investigation and his wife's nervous breakdown. Moon also has a problem with his wife. Just before he sits down to write, Jane is swept off by Malquist for a midnight punting expedition. The Risen Christ has, ironically enough, fallen over after drinking too much creme de menthe. Moon, the actor in this domestic drama as well as the spectator of it, has just killed the General for taking pornographic pictures of Marie. To round things off, his notes are burnt by the electric fire. Moon is prone to a whole series of accidents throughout the novel which leave him comically wounded and mutilated. The irony is that, as a historian, he believes that nothing happens accidentally. He gets round the problem of his missing notes by deciding to invent them. Stoppard suggests that all writers, including biographers and historians, are liars. As will be shown, this becomes a major theme in *Travesties*. Moon sets about doctoring one of Malquist's letters so that it reads as if it was part of their conversation at their first meeting. After he has struggled to produce this fiction which will be passed off as history, a letter arrives enclosing Malquist's cheque which has bounced. Patrons, like writers, are also liars.

Moon is very similar to Ros and Guil. He is an archetypal little man who becomes involved in events which are beyond his control. He desperately seeks meaning and refuses to believe that chaos and accident may be the only explanations. Yet, insofar as there is destiny, he is destined to be disappointed in his quest because he is always capable of contradicting any point of view. Malquist's coachman, O'Hara, presents a problem. His name suggests that he is Irish, although he confuses matters by talking with a Jewish accent. Stoppard jumbles everything up together including the stereotypes. O'Hara, unseen on top of the coach, eventually turns out to be a negro. This is just one of the ambushes that Stoppard springs. Long John Slaughter is revealed to be more Sloane ranger than lone ranger. As identity is usually no more than a theatrical mask, it can be fluid and interchangeable. Moon's initial response to being ambushed by O'Hara's identity takes the form of a racist tirade. He then checks himself and apologizes:

But I take both parts, O'Hara, leapfrogging myself along the great moral issues, refuting myself and rebutting the refutation towards a truth that must be a compound of two opposite half-truths. And you never reach it because there is always something more to say.   (p. 53)

Like Guil and Stoppard himself, Moon can never find the last word because he is always aware of the contradictions to it. As indicated, this also prevents him from writing very many of the first words as well.

The similarities between *Rosencrantz* and *Malquist* show that Stoppard pirates his own material as well as that of other writers. He can be, to pirate a phrase, a bubonic plagiarist. The same lines occur in both works and characters are drawn along the same lines. Like Ros and Guil, Moon enjoys a good game. He has to play with himself since everybody else is too preoccupied to join in. He is even reduced on one occasion to interviewing himself to find out whether he is schizophrenic! He plays the parts of both Ros and Guil in these attempts to grasp at straws of meaning. His confusion is also given specifically childlike qualities. Despite his attempts to become a serious historian, he remains the little boy lost. Things go wrong when he moves from being a bewildered spectator to a man of action. He carries a bomb around with him because he thinks that a big bang is necessary. This grand gesture backfires comically on him. When the bomb finally explodes during the funeral procession, it only releases a large balloon with 'a two-word message – familiar, unequivocal and obscene' (p. 165). The big bang turns into a schoolboy's whimper: confused obscenities over national institutions and monuments. *Rosencrantz* may inscribe a more elegant version of grafitti on the cultural monument of *Hamlet*, but *Malquist* chalks up some good jokes on the tomb of the heroic in history.

Malquist is an erratic novel. It is nevertheless worth considering because of its close relationship to *Rosencrantz*. Its theme of writing about writing is also developed in many of Stoppard's later works. Stoppard plays games with his readers in much the same way as he teases his audiences. Perhaps these games would have been more successful if he had constructed rather than merely implied a reader or readers. Italo Calvino's *If on a Winter's Night a Traveller* (1981) is able to play more sophisticated metafictional games through the construction of a male and a female reader, whose responses to fiction become the fiction.

Given Stoppard's insistence that there are always at least two sides to every coin, it would be dangerous to label him as either a Malquist or a Moon. Moon, the confused liberal, is at the centre of the novel because his centre of consciousness is the only one to which the reader is granted sustained access. Malquist, the reactionary dandy, is nevertheless provided with the most memorable lines. Stylistically, Stoppard is a dandy who self-consciously shows off both his new and borrowed clothes. This is the exclusive spectacle that we mere spectators are offered. Intellectually, he shares some of the liberal confusion of the ordinary person which characterizes Moon as well as Ros and Guil. This dandy expends a great deal of his stylistic energy on seemingly expendable people.

Parody as camp

Susan Sontag indicates that such a potential paradox is the essence of camp. *Malquist*, like many of Stoppard's other works, highlights the problem of how to be a dandy in an age of mass culture. Malquist's own solution, as suggested, is to pretend that such vulgarity does not exist. The alternative, or camp, solution is for the dandy to become a connoisseur of bad taste. He can, paradoxically, only retain exclusivity by being inclusive. Camp is therefore both exclusively aristocratic as well as being inclusively democratic. It is attached to bad taste while remaining detached from it. The modern dandy does not need to dismiss either mass-produced genre fiction like Regency romances or mass-produced people like Moon as being too vulgar. He can develop instead what Sontag calls 'a good taste of bad taste', which ultimately leads to the favourite camp position that only the unspeakably 'awful' is worth speaking about. The emphasis on 'good taste' retains the exclusive position, while introduction of 'bad taste' draws attention to the inclusive one.

Camp does not represent a complete break with old-style dandyism. As will be apparent, it can only define itself through paradoxes. It asserts that surface is the only substance and that heightened theatricality is the only reality. These are all characteristics which modern dandies like Stoppard share with their predecessors. All dandies hold up a mirror to themselves, yet the modern one also holds this mirror up to less aesthetically pleasing spectacles. He affects to believe that artistic failure represents success and that only the naïve can be truly sophisticated. He is thus fascinated by stereotypes, or by what Sontag calls 'instant character':

What Camp taste responds to is 'instant character' . . . and, conversely, what it is not stirred by is the sense of the development of character. Character is understood as a state of continual incandescence – a person being one, very intense thing.

As argued in the analysis of *Rosencrantz*, Stoppard is only stirred by the idea of character development because he wants to ambush it. Ros and Guil are instant characters in the sense that, as attendant lords, they are Renaissance stereotypes. Stoppard may upset the conventions by allowing them to dominate his play, but they only do so as modern stereotypes. The Player plays a variety of instant characters in an 'intense', or highly theatrical, manner. The appeal of the stereotype for the modern dandy is that it does not disguise, or understate, its theatricality. Joan Collins, the super-bitch in *Dynasty*, has become a camp cult because there is never any doubt about the fact that she is acting, and indeed over-acting, a part which is based on just one characteristic. Her shoulders may be padded out but her psychology is not. Stoppard plays around with stereotypes in *Malquist*. He is not satirizing them for their tastelessness. He is, rather, parodying them as part of a camp statement about his 'good taste' in 'bad taste'. The quantity of these parodies may be related to Sontag's point that 'the hallmark of camp is the spirit of extravagance'. Nothing succeeds like excess.

The Real Inspector Hound

The Real Inspector Hound, which was first performed at the Criterion in 1968, is one of Stoppard's many variations on the overlapping themes of parody and ambush. As the title suggests, this one-act play plays with the conventions of the detective or whodunit genre. Whereas *Rosencrantz* parodied a specific play, *Hound* targets a genre. The references range from the Sherlock Holmes stories through to contemporary whodunits. *Hound* is not, however, a medley of parodies in the manner of *Malquist*. It is, rather, a well-constructed and tightly controlled work. This control is achieved through a specific concentration on the stage versions of Agatha Christie's stories. The more discursive references are subordinated to this central concern with Christie's particular brand of English country house murder.

Stoppard is, once again, leading a playful assault on a rival national institution. Christie's play *The Mousetrap* (1952) had been running, or as some said standing still, in the West End for over fifteen years before *Hound* cheekily arrived to send it up. It was still very much there after Stoppard's take-off was taken off. As a popular West End production, *The Mousetrap* already had a status which approached that of *Hamlet* in the classical repertoire. *Hound* parodies a number of Christie's other plays as well, for instance *The Unexpected Guest* (1958) which is also set at a fogbound country house. A brief summary of the parallels between Stoppard's play and *The Mousetrap* will nevertheless suggest the nature, if not the scope, of his parody.

Policemen or supposed policemen make dramatic entrances in both plays. Hound enters wearing enormous swamp boots and carrying a foghorn, whereas Sergeant Trotter first appears on skis in *The Mousetrap*. Such equipment is necessary because of the bad weather that has all but cut off the main locations from the outside world. Stoppard's Muldoon Manor is always unreachable at high tide and is surrounded by dense fog, whereas Christie's Monkswell Manor is isolated after a particularly heavy fall of snow. Information about the weather, and other matters, is conveyed in both plays by the radio, which is very conveniently switched on at just the right moments. Telephone conversations are also used in both as a way of imparting stage directions to the audience.

Stoppard borrows freely from Christie. In every case, however, he overstates her themes and dramatic devices. Trotter's entrance on skis is plausible enough given the weather conditions. It is only retrospectively that it appears as odd. When Hound enters, however, such a concern for plausibility is thrown out of the French windows:

Enter INSPECTOR HOUND. *On his feet are his swamp boots. These are two*

*inflatable – and inflated – pontoons with flat bottoms about two feet across. He
carries a foghorn.* (p. 30)

Stoppard inflates Christie. Such overstatement is neatly contrasted with
Hound's understated responses. He modestly mentions that 'It takes
more than a bit of weather to keep a policeman from his duty' (p. 30).
Although he nearly gives the game away at one point by advising a
telephone call to the police, he manages to play the part of the reserved
detective with some success. He trips over the corpse and then asks
everybody whether there is anything they have forgotten to tell him.
Stoppard parodied flat-footed detectives who are unable to nose out
what is under their noses again in *Jumpers* (1972), where Inspector Bones
just misses catching a glimpse of McFee's body. The device is a common
one in parodies of the police. It is used even more effectively by Orton in
Loot (1967).

   The Mousetrap opens with a radio message about a murder in London.
This is followed by a weather report. Stoppard's whodunit opens with
the same creaking piece of scene setting, which is used, or rather over-
used, throughout:

... Inspector Hound who is masterminding the operation is not available for
comment but it is widely believed that he has a secret plan ... Meanwhile police
and volunteers are combing the swamps with loud-hailers, shouting, 'Don't be a
madman, give yourself up.' That is the end of the police message. (p. 18)

This particular coin has a policeman on one side and a lunatic on the
other. Stoppard also parodies the use of telephone calls in whodunits.
Mrs Drudge, the daily help, very stagily delivers stage directions to
callers who have got the wrong number. She is a close theatrical relation
of Mrs Swabb in Alan Bennett's *Habeas Corpus* (1973) and Mrs Clackett
in Michael Frayn's *Noises Off* (1982). The cue for the telephone calls is
invariably late, so Mrs Drudge has to hover in anticipation. Stoppard,
like both Bennett and Frayn, parodies the production techniques, or the
lack of them, associated with provincial theatre. The dialogue is as
awkward as the staging. Simon Gascoyne is bowled over by Uncle
Magnus's wheelchair and lies unconscious. He is asked to say something
to prove that he is still alive. He proves that he has not forgotten his
country house manners when he replies 'I'm most frightfully sorry'
(p. 23).

   Stoppard twists the tail of the whodunit to make it absurd. The revelations at the end of *The Mousetrap* are relatively straightforward ones.

Sergeant Trotter turns out to be Georgie, the murderer, whereas Major Metcalf is the real policeman. The detective who is not all that he appears to be is a convention of the genre. Inspector Goole in J. B. Priestley's *An Inspector Calls* (1945) creates as much mystery as he solves. Stoppard piles unlikely revelation on top of, or rather over the top of, unlikely revelation. Uncle Magnus turns out to be that old favourite, the policeman who is a master of disguise. Orton also had fun with this by making Truscott masquerade as an employee of the Water Board. Magnus leaps out of his wheelchair, strips off his false moustaches and announces that he is the real Inspector Hound. He also just happens to be Lady Cynthia Muldoon's long-lost husband:

Yes! – it is me, Albert! – who lost his memory and joined the force, rising by merit to the rank of Inspector, his past blotted out – until fate cast him back into the home he left behind, back to the beautiful woman he had brought here as his girlish bride – in short, my darling, my memory has returned and your long wait is over!   (p. 48)

Here and elsewhere Stoppard includes his own comic themes, for instance loss of memory. Yet the overall comic effect is achieved by inflating Christie's own material.

Stoppard's jokes are invariably at least triple-decker ones. Ken Tynan once complained that a scene in *Travesties* was 'a triple-decker bus that isn't going anywhere'. The Magnus/Hound/Albert character provides *Hound* with a triple-decker ending. Stoppard adds another deck, or layer, by revealing that this character is being played by Puckeridge, who is a third-string drama critic or 'stand-in's stand-in' (p. 19). Once again, an attendant lord figure has been placed at the centre of the stage. The significance of this revelation only becomes apparent when the parody of Christie is related to the parody of theatrical reviewers which frames it. Stoppard has claimed that the play is not about theatre reviewers. They just happen to be easily identifiable members of a theatre audience. Such special pleading does not need to be taken too seriously. Stoppard teases the theatre reviewers, although is careful in his remarks about the play to avoid the risk of alienating them.

As the stage directions indicate, the first thing that the theatre audience sees is a 'reflection' (p. 9) of itself. Stoppard's theatre holds the mirror up to itself rather than to nature. Two reviewers, Moon and Birdboot, settle down upstage to watch the production of the whodunit that is set at Muldoon Manor. The actor–spectator coin is being flipped over again. Moon and Birdboot act out the parts of spectators taking their seats in the theatre: flicking impatiently through the programme, munching chocolates and trying to impress each other. Moon belongs to the pseudo-intellectual school of theatre reviewers. He affects to be a man of letters rather than a man of the theatre. He searches for hidden symbolic or psychological meanings and also likes to show off his literary credentials by reeling off a string of important names in a desperate attempt to establish a context for the whodunit. Stoppard is having a dig at those critics, academics as well as journalists, whose pedantic response to *Rosencrantz* was to list all its conceivable, and inconceivable, sources. Moon's style of reviewing, with its awkward rhetorical questions and knowing little tags, completely misses the point of a pointless play:

Let me at once say that it has *élan* while at the same time avoiding *éclat*. Having said that, and I think it must be said, I am bound to ask – does this play know where it is going . . . Does it, I repeat, declare its affiliations? . . . *Je suis*, it seems to be saying, *ergo sum*. But is that enough? I think we are entitled to ask. (p. 28)

Birdboot, on the other hand, is a man of the theatre who affects to know instinctively and intuitively the kind of rattling good show that the great British public really wants. Whereas Moon's reviewing is close to Guil's advice to the Player, Birdboot's views on theatrical form and content are similar to those expressed by Ros:

. . . The groundwork has been well and truly laid, and the author has taken the trouble to learn from the masters of the genre. He has created a real situation, and few will doubt his ability to resolve it with a startling denouement. Certainly that is what it so far lacks, but it has a beginning, a middle and I have no doubt it will prove to have an end. For this let us give thanks, and double thanks for a good clean show without a trace of smut . . . (p. 35)

These reviews, which are being self-importantly composed while the performance is in progress, are both ridiculously wide of the mark. Birdboot's self-appointed role as custodian of public morality is undercut by the way in which he lusts after nearly every actress he sees. He knows much more about discreet hotels run by men of the world than he does about the theatre or the great British public.

Moon is obsessed by the fact that he is only the second-string critic, whereas Birdboot tries to reconcile public morality with his own private immorality. Their conversations both before and during the performance therefore tend to take the form of overlapping monologues. Stoppard's parody is directed specifically at theatre reviewers, although it also serves as a playful critique of a chattering, inattentive theatre audience in

97

general. Moon and Birdboot act out their fantasies while the play stumbles along: Moon dreams of being a first-string critic and Birdboot imagines adding another actress to his string of them. Their self-obsessions lead them to become actors in the whodunit. The telephone rings on stage during one of the intervals. This seems at first to be the result of the appalling stage management which has characterized the production. The call turns out, however, to be from Mrs Birdboot, who is checking up to make sure that her husband has not disappeared to one of his discreet hotels. It now appears likely, insofar as anything is meant to be likely, that some of the earlier calls might have come from her as well. Birdboot takes the call and is ambushed on stage by the return of the cast. He finds himself involved in a re-run of the first act. As a spectator he had followed the same path as Simon Gascoyne: transferring his affections from Felicity to Lady Cynthia Muldoon. As an actor he now finds himself playing the part of Simon. Spectators and actors are different sides of the same coin. Birdboot's fantasies are now realized. He rejects Felicity and declares his love for Cynthia. This pleasurable dream turns into a nightmare as Birdboot, along with the rest of the audience, already knows that the script demands that the Simon Gascoyne character is murdered. Like Ros and Guil, Birdboot is trapped by theatrical events beyond his control. It is written that he has to be murdered. He is murdered.

It is now Moon's turn to become an actor in this apology for a drama. He leaves his seat to investigate the murder of his friend. He is also concerned to establish why the body that Hound tripped over should be that of Higgs, the first-string reviewer. He is therefore cast as Hound when he too is ambushed by the actors. He is unable to escape back to the safety of his seat because the actors who have been playing Simon and Hound are now occupying the reviewers' places. Simon, who was murdered on stage, is nevertheless shown to be alive and well. Like *Rosencrantz, Hound* draws attention to the illusion of stage death. Simon and Hound now play the parts of the reviewers. Although their observations contain some of the terms and phrases used by Moon and Birdboot, their response is a much more critical one. It is only when actors and spectators have changed places that the play is described accurately as 'A complete ragbag' (p. 44). Moon makes a slow and painful start in his new role as Inspector Hound. Although both he and Birdboot set themselves up as arbiters of theatrical taste, they start out as clumsy actors even in comparison with a clumsy cast. Moon eventually gets into the swing of the part. So the actor–spectator coin produces another variation: just as the actors make better reviewers than the reviewers, so Moon eventually becomes a better actor than the actors. He tenaciously pursues the play's obligatory red herring, which members of the theatre audience ought to be able to smell more than a mile off. This concerns the activities of the real McCoy, a mysterious Canadian with a grudge. It is based on Christie's *The Unexpected Guest*, in which the murderer turns out to be a Canadian with a grudge called MacGregor. Moon is unmasked while he is trying to unmask the killer by the unmasked Hound. Hound, no longer impersonating Magnus, accuses Moon of impersonating Hound. Stoppard has never been a fan of the neat denouement or last word, so he parodies the convention with this bewilderingly neat conclusion. Moon has dreamt of killing Higgs, the first-string critic, and that is enough to convict him as a 'madman' and a 'killer' (p. 47). Puckeridge may have been acting the parts of Magnus, the real Inspector Hound and Lord Muldoon, but he is also the villain of the piece. He has a grudge against both Higgs and Moon because they are higher up the journalistic ladder. He therefore feels no qualms about shooting Moon when he tries to escape from his nightmare. Puckeridge now has the opportunity to camp it up at the Old Vic in an opera cloak.

Like most parodies of the whodunit, *Hound* is meant to be confusing. To take just one other example, Michael Palin's Ripping Yarn about *Murder at Moorstones Manor* (1977) has an equally absurd denouement in which almost everybody queues up to confess to murder. As suggested, there are a number of interesting parallels between *Hound* and *Rosencrantz*. They both parody other well-known plays. They both rescue second- and third-stringers from oblivion. They comment on themselves and on theatricality in general. Distinctions between actors and spectators are questioned and reversed. Both plays show spectators, or would-be spectators, getting caught up in theatrical events which are beyond their control. Last, and by no means least, they are both very funny. Stoppard inflates Christie only to deflate her. He continues to parody the whodunit in *Jumpers*, *After Magritte* and, as will be shown, *Dogg's Hamlet, Cahoot's Macbeth* (1979). He also parodies the related genre of spy fiction in one of his radio plays, *The Dog It Was That Died* (1982).

Some other genre parodists

Tynan's account of *Show People* (1980) includes profiles of both Stoppard and Mel Brooks. The only explicit connection that he offers between them is that they are among the very select band of show business people whom he would invite to his ideal dinner party. Stoppard and Brooks would have plenty to talk about at a dinner party since they are both inveterate parodists. Like *Hound*, many of Brooks's films are based upon genre parody. *Blazing Saddles* (1974) is an unaffectionate parody, often shading over into a satire, of Hollywood Westerns. The parodies are more affectionate in *Young Frankenstein* (1974), *Silent Movie* (1976) and *High Anxiety* (1977). Brooks's films, like Stoppard's plays, also draw attention to artistic processes and practices in more explicit ways. *The Producers* (1967) deals with an unsuccessful attempt to stage a Broadway disaster. It therefore concentrates on theatrical patronage, dress rehearsals and audience reactions to the first night performance. Like Stoppard, Brooks shows his audiences a reflection of themselves. *Blazing Saddles* ends with confusion at the film studios between the actors in this parody Western and the cast of a Busby Berkeley musical. The audience is reminded that it is not just watching a film about other films, but also a film about filming. Most of the action in *Silent Movie* concerns the attempts by a production team to cast a number of stars in the silent movie, which represents the film within the film. Although Brooks's brand of comedy tends to be whackier than Stoppard's, they both derive some of their best effects by juxtaposing the conventional with the colloquial. Brooks, for instance, often uses modern Jewish jokes in the most unlikely historical settings. Ros does exactly the same at one point in *Rosencrantz* (p. 52). Brooks's genre parodies depend for their success on a more extended version of this kind of comic clash. The Broadway musical is parodied in *The Producers* through the clash between the form and content of *Springtime for Hitler*. Shows and spectaculars are also treated irreverently in *History of the World – Part I* (1981) in which the section on the Spanish Inquisition includes an underwater ballet sequence performed by nuns. This is a more outrageous version of the clash between the contemporary and the Renaissance in *Rosencrantz*. As will be suggested, *Travesties* sets up a wide variety of clashes between form and content, notably through locating serious twentieth-century debates within a comic Victorian framework.

Genre parodies have dominated recent television and radio comedy. As implied during the discussion of the third act of *Rosencrantz*, *I'm Sorry I'll Read That Again* parodied the conventions associated with other radio programmes. Its title draws attention to one particular radio cliché. *Monty Python's Flying Circus* parodied a wide variety of television formats: quiz shows, interviews, announcements, sports reports, nature programmes, historical documentaries, to name but a few of them. It also parodied other forms of television comedy, particularly those which offered a series of self-contained sketches which were each rounded off with a punchline. A familiar running joke in *Python* was the collapsing of various sketches into one another and the refusal to provide any of them with punchlines. Such transgressions of the conventions were often explicitly drawn attention to by authority-figures, who interrupted the proceedings to try to get the cast to put on a good clean show with a beginning, a middle and end. Like both *Rosencrantz* and *Hound*, *Python* reviewed itself and drew attention to its own theatricality. Such interruptions offered a particularly good way of ambushing conventions which sought to disguise rather than reveal their artificiality. The opening moments of the Ripping Yarn of *Whinfrey's Last Case* (1979) contain another kind of interruption, which ambushes a particular style of television narration. A very famous personality tries to set the scene by evoking mood and period atmosphere outside a London house. His seemingly naturalistic address to the audience is nevertheless revealed to be a self-consciously artificial piece to camera by the way in which it is broken into by sights and sounds from the street. The production assistant is unable to prevent a meat porter and a traveller in underwear from getting in on the act. The question of how to 'act natural' is playfully posed.

Styles of narration are also part of Richard O'Brien's genre parodies of science fiction and horror films in *The Rocky Horror Show* (1973). An Edgar Lustgarten figure, well played by Charles Gray in the film version, offers a series of impressive sounding but meaningless linking commentaries. O'Brien's parody, like Stoppard's one in *Hound*, depends on the accumulative effect of the clichés. The narrator does not have to be ambushed to make a point about theatricality because he continually ambushes himself with his own rhetoric. Frank-n-Furter also speaks only in movie clichés:

Everything looks black, the chips are down ... Your back is against the wall. You panic – you're trapped – there's no way out and even if there was it would probably be a one-way ticket to the bottom of the bay. And then suddenly you get a break – all the pieces seem to fit into place – what a sucker you'd been – what a fool – the answer was there all the time – it took a small accident to make it happen.

This medley of clichés, which sends itself up, may be compared with, say, Uncle Magnus's speech at the end of *Hound*. It may also be related to speeches like Ros's 'To accost, or not to accost' one in *Rosencrantz*, even though this is a general parody rather than a specific genre one. *Rocky Horror*, which parodies popular music as well as films, tends to offer a much more explicit version of camp than Stoppard's works do. Such differences of emphasis should not, however, disguise the fact that, as parodists, Stoppard and O'Brien have much in common. *Rocky Horror* juxtaposes the traditional 1950s morality found in feature films with early 1970s narcissism, transvestitism and 'trans-sexuality'. Brad, Janet, Dr Scott, Eddie and the Narrator all represent this traditional morality. They find themselves in a world in which the rules of their particular genre (and gender) do not apply. This represents a variation on the theme of *Rosencrantz* in which modern characters find themselves, through a time warp, back in the world of *Hamlet*.

Genre parodies increase and multiply. The film *Dead Men Don't Wear Plaid* (1983) to some extent carried on where *Hound* left off, although the parody is more specifically of private eye movies rather than country house whodunits. The whole approach of *Comic Strip Presents . . .* is based on genre parody. To take just one example, a package holiday to Spain is shot in the style of a Sergio Leone spaghetti Western. Rowan Atkinson is perhaps the parodist whose work most closely resembles what Stoppard did in *Rosencrantz*. The *Black Adder* television programmes place him first of all back in the world of Shakespeare's English history plays and then in Elizabethan England itself. This sets up possibilities for clashes between the ancient and the modern. Atkinson has a range of very modern gestures and facial expressions which are meant to be out of place in a period drama. Ros and Guil should be played in the same way.

6. *Travesties* and Metadrama

Setting the scene

It was probably inevitable that Stoppard should eventually write a play in which loss of memory is the controlling device rather than just one of the running jokes. Much of *Travesties*, which was first performed at the Aldwych in 1974, is filtered through the erratic memory of the elderly Henry Carr. Stoppard rescues, once again, a central character from obscurity. Just as Ros and Guil are moved out from the margins of *Hamlet*, so Carr becomes more than just a literary footnote. His only claim to fame was that he had taken the part of Algernon in a production of Oscar Wilde's *The Importance of Being Earnest*, for which James Joyce had acted as business manager. Records of this production might have sunk without a trace had it not been for the legal action which followed it. Carr demanded payment for the clothes that he had had to buy to cut a suitably sartorial figure as Algernon, whereas Joyce argued that Carr owed him money for tickets. Angry words were exchanged and the case went to court, which was most unlike the home life of Algernon. Carr lost the legal battle and, to add insult to injury, found himself being caricatured by Joyce in *Ulysses* (1922). He was therefore assured of the dubious distinction of becoming a scholarly footnote. *Travesties* represents his revenge since he gets his own back by caricaturing Joyce.

Switzerland's neutrality during the First World War meant that it provided a safe bed for some strange fellows. Other writers besides Joyce were attracted by its peace and calm. Lenin came to Zurich to write his analysis of imperialism. It also provided a haven for the writers associated rather freely with Dadaism. They were anti-writers since, among other things, they wanted to destroy essentially romantic conceptions of the privileged positions of both art and artists. They were also against history in any shape or form, declaring that it was irrelevant to know whether there had been other people before them. Tristan Tzara, the Rumanian poet, playwright and propagandist, becomes their representative in *Travesties*.

The fact that Joyce, Lenin and Tzara were all in Zurich at more or less the same time offers Stoppard a golden opportunity to write, once again, about writers and writing. A fourth writer is added to the scenario by making Carr into a biographer and memoirist. Stoppard clearly believes that nothing succeeds like excess. The fifth writer is Oscar Wilde himself. Carr considers himself to have been such a success as Algernon that he asserts his own importance by reconstructing all other events in terms of this one event. He casts both Joyce and Tzara, but significantly not Lenin, as parts in *The Importance*, which therefore provides the structuring device for his memories. It seems as though life is being made to imitate art. Yet, although Carr shapes his life in terms of Wilde's play, this life is in turn shaped by Stoppard's play. Art therefore imitates art in the same self-referential manner as it does in *Rosencrantz, Malquist* and *Hound*.

Carr gives the part of Jack to Tristan Tzara, possibly because it was originally played in Zurich by a Tristan Rawson. Joyce is cast as Lady Augusta Bracknell, perhaps because he was christened erroneously as James Augusta Joyce. Gwendolen is played by Carr's sister and Cecily by a librarian who eventually becomes his wife. There is, as indicated, some method in the madness of Carr's casting. Joyce's artistic self-importance is well matched by Lady Bracknell's social self-esteem. Tzara was a dandy and therefore not a bad choice for Jack. *Travesties* is designed, however, to set up oppositions rather than similarities. A great modernist writer is made to play a philistine society hostess. A man takes the woman's part. A cosmopolitan artistic revolutionary is cast as an English gentleman of leisure who is dedicated to pleasure. Such oppositions produce the clashes between form and content which characterize *Travesties*. Wilde's urbane, witty dialogue is, for instance, an inappropriate vehicle for the content of Dadaist manifestos. Tynan suggests that Stoppard is a bad driver because his multi-decker bus of a play travels in different directions at the same time. Yet only a very good driver could do this. *Travesties* is a piece of metadrama which seeks to show, and show off, how form and content can pull in a variety of different directions.

Stoppard makes no bones of the fact that he usually needs the bones of another play to provide him with a structure. He prefers plotting dialogue and ambushes to plotting plays. Just as John Fowles bounces his own novel off a Victorian one in *The French Lieutenant's Woman* (1969), so Stoppard juxtaposes the contemporary with the Victorian. *The Importance*, like both *Hamlet* and *The Mousetrap*, is a play which bears its reputation before it. As Linda Hutcheon has demonstrated, parody is paradoxical. At one level it is essentially conservative because it reinforces dominant cultural assumptions about art. To put the point crudely, only parodies of what is either highly regarded (*Hamlet*) or highly popular (*The Mousetrap*) can ever work. At another level, however, parody can be subversive because it challenges the traditional ways in which either great or popular texts are perceived and received. Parody is therefore a mixture of reverence and irreverence. It depends for its success on a recognition and repetition of approved cultural definitions and traditions, while at the same time providing a context in which they become unrecognizable and unfamiliar. In Hutcheon's terms, parody is both the 'custodian of artistic legacy' and the authorized transgressor of this legacy. Stoppard chooses what has become a classic play to provide the framework for *Travesties*, yet by using it in this way he denies as well as affirms its classic status.

Travesties differs from Stoppard's other parodies in that it is almost essential to know *The Importance*, and to a lesser extent *Ulysses*, very well in order to appreciate the metadrama. This is not the case with *Rosencrantz*. Stoppard's more caviar jokes may be lost on spectators who only have a sketchy knowledge of *Hamlet*. The play is still accessible and, to flip the coin over, it can be an asset to share some of Ros and Guil's confusions at the comings and goings of the Danish court. Detailed knowledge of the plays which are being parodied is also an optional extra in *Hound* and *Dirty Linen*. It could be argued that any confusion on the part of the spectators about Stoppard's use of *The Importance* is appropriate for a play which is about confusion. *Travesties* deals with confusions of memory, tone, identity and ideological analysis. Confused spectators are just part of the parcel which Stoppard wraps up for this particular party game. It can also be argued that the repetition of particular scenes from *The Importance* allows spectators to familiarize themselves with it while they are also watching Stoppard's play. Yet a prior knowledge of Wilde is still essential in order to appreciate the particular nature of the confusions which are built up around Cecily in the second half of *Travesties*.

It is easy enough, however, to see in more general terms the function of Wilde's play. It becomes, like Zurich during the Great War, an island of calm amid a sea of troubles. This calm is shown to be very precarious. Carr reconstructs events along the lines of *The Importance*, yet its well-wrought structure is ultimately unable to contain the social and intellectual upheavals of the period. There are thus frequent clashes between Wilde's pleasantries and the unpleasant facts associated with the war. The problem with this general representation of *The Importance* is that it overlooks the play's own statements of ideological conflict. For instance,

Wilde was making an important point about Victorian double standards through Jack's double identity. Jack has one identity for pleasure and another for duty. This essentially theatrical practice was also followed by many Victorian men. The representation of *The Importance* as a neutral country in an ideological war, rather than as a critique of Victorian values, offers a travesty of Wilde.

Act One

Like *Rosencrantz*, *Travesties* immediately presents the audience with a puzzle. Unnamed characters indulge in bizarre activities. The character who is eventually revealed to be Tzara cuts up a poem, shakes the fragments around in his hat and then reads out his re-arranged version of it. It is, in English anyway, nonsense poetry. The character who is eventually revealed to be Joyce dictates virtually incomprehensible fragments of *Ulysses* to Gwendolen. A character who is unmistakably Lenin is also shown to be writing on scraps of paper. He then discusses the outbreak of the Russian Revolution, in Russian, with his wife. The three writers work simultaneously but independently of each other. An English-speaking audience might think at first that the location is the Tower of Babel, although it turns out to be the Zurich Public Library. Libraries offer ideal settings for writers like Stoppard who write about writing: David Lodge's *The British Museum is Falling Down* (1965) and the ending of Calvino's *If on a Winter's Night a Traveller* are just two more examples of this kind of self-reflexive placing. Indeed, when the opening of *Travesties* is considered on the page rather than the stage it provides quite clear statements about itself. The play, maybe itself no more than a fragment, will collect together these other fragmentary pieces of writing. The isolation of three writers suggests the clashes and oppositions that are to follow. Such interpretations should not, however, be allowed to play down the confusion which is played up in this opening scene.

Stoppard then reveals that this scene is itself a fragment, or figment, of old Carr's muddled brain. Carr stops the action because it has roller-coastered out of his control. Stoppard describes Carr's wandering memory, and thus narration, in terms of a toy train that jumps the rails and has to be re-started. The metaphor is not a random one since it provides another illustration of how Stoppard relates his plays to childhood games. It may also be helpful to consider other contexts for this kind of narration. *Travesties* suggests that history, far from being an authentic account of the past, is a photograph which is continually edited or re-touched. Carr can therefore be seen as editing the snapshots related to his life, stopping and then starting again until each one tells the right story. Another way of representing the process is to see him, like the narrator of *Malquist*, as an erratic projectionist, who keeps on editing and re-winding the reel which contains his life story.

Carr is a mixture of Malquist and Moon. He shares Malquist's dandyism and, like Moon, sets himself up in the 'posterity' business by trying to recall the great men with whom he has rubbed his well-tailored shoulders. His problem here is that, as the quintessential Englishman abroad, he regards all foreigners as being funny. This explains the caricature versions of Tzara, Joyce and Lenin with which the play so confusingly opened. Carr is unable to produce a reverential account of his friendship with Joyce because they were not friends:

– in short, a complex personality, an enigma, a contradictory spokesman for the truth, an obsessive litigant and yet an essentially private man who wished his total indifference to public notice to be universally recognised – in short a liar and a hypocrite, a tight-fisted, sponging, fornicating drunk not worth the paper, that's that bit done. (p. 23)

The clichés associated with literary reminiscences clash with Carr's animosity towards the great man. Carr has no more success with a book entitled *Lenin As I Knew Him*, presumably modelled on Nikolay Valentinov's *Encounters with Lenin* (1968), because it rapidly becomes apparent that the title itself is a lie. Like Moon, Carr attempts to pass off fiction as fact. *Travesties* obviously draws its inspiration from Wilde's 'The Decay of Lying' as well as from *The Importance*. Carr dignifies himself with the title of 'Carr of the Consulate', but is unable to sustain the necessary heroic tone. He is not Lawrence of Arabia, nor was meant to be. His guide-book opening to another piece of writing which is destined to remain in the bottom drawer of his mind, *Street of Revolution! A Sketch*, quickly degenerates into asides about Swiss brothels. *Memories of Dada by a Consular Friend of the Famous in Old Zurich: A Sketch* confirms that memory lane is not a straight and narrow path.

The only event that 'Carr of the Consulate' is an authority on is his own performance as Algernon. He therefore sets aside his fragmentary memoirs and sketches and plunges into his own version of *The Importance*. He cues in Bennett, who is given the part of Lane, with the tea tray and Stoppard's audience is plunged into the opening of Wilde's play. The Zurich Public Library is replaced by Half Moon Street. Clothes are the main topic of conversation. Carr, now transformed into a young man, declares that he would feel absolutely naked if he went to the theatre without 'the straight cut trouser with the blue satin stripe and the silk cutaway' (p. 26). Stoppard is playing with the actor–spectator coin again by drawing attention to the way in which spectators, like actors, dress up to play a part. He also emphasizes the way in which Carr is dressing up events and his part in them. The re-run of Wilde's play allows Carr, literally and metaphorically, to fashion his younger self.

This opening scene is played several times. Such breaks in continuity, which obviously ambush spectators who expect linear narratives, can be interpreted in terms of old Carr's memory wandering off and then coming back with a jolt to the starting point. The important question must be whether he is trying to remember art or life. He is, at one level, an old actor who is no longer able to remember all of his lines. It is therefore possible to take the starting and stopping of the action as another example of metadrama in *Travesties*. It becomes more and more apparent that Carr is not in fact concerned with facts. For example, it turns out that Bennett was his superior at the Consulate rather than his butler. It therefore makes sense to see these breaks in continuity as being caused by his lack of artistic invention. He is a failed writer as well as a failed actor. He is trying to play a language game rather than reconstruct the past. Just as Ros and Guil conducted imaginary conversations with Hamlet or the King of England, so Carr attempts to construct a series of such conversations within the framework of *The Importance*. This means that the theatrical pace of *Travesties* is similar to that of *Rosencrantz*: bouts of intense activity while a language game is in progress followed by quite significant pauses until a substitute becomes available. Like Ros and Guil, Carr plays this stop–go game to pass the time. It is a convenient piece of shorthand to describe his narration as the product of an erratic memory. It is more accurate, however, to see it as the product of an erratic imagination. Perhaps memory and imagination are just different sides of the same coin anyway.

Carr may begin his version of *The Importance* by being in control, but he quickly loses the initiative to Bennett. Wilde's Algernon is bored by references to his butler's family life. A variation of this theme occurs in *Travesties*:

CARR (*languidly*):   I'm not sure that I'm much interested in your views, Bennett.
BENNETT (*apologetically*):   They're *not* particularly interesting, sir.   (p. 31)

The new context for this kind of exchange travesties the original one. It is set in the middle of Bennett's detailed and well-informed analysis of the causes of the Russian Revolution. First of all, the comedy is achieved by even introducing such a topic into a late Victorian drawing-room. Secondly, the servant rather than the master is in control. Wilde certainly sketches in this theme, although Stoppard chooses to emphasize it. Thirdly, and this is the comic effect in which Stoppard is really interested, the analysis of the Russian Revolution is delivered in an impassive tone which is entirely appropriate for a stage butler. The explication of class exploitation bears no relation to its mode of delivery. Here, and throughout the play, Stoppard ambushes the audience by upsetting conventional expectations about relationships between form and content. Inconsistency is all he asks for, which, in the paradoxical world which both he and Wilde inhabit, is the only true kind of consistency.

Carr gives up with Bennett and cues in Tzara to play Jack Worthing. A comic foreigner struts on to act the part of an English gentleman: 'Plaizure, plaizure! What else? Eating ez usual, I see 'Enri?!' (p. 32). This scene rapidly gets out of Carr's control as he continues to caricature foreigners. Joyce, playing Lady Bracknell, spouts Irish limericks and soon everybody else is at it as well. Wilde's dialogue has been praised for its musical cadences and operatic rhythms. It becomes in this new context the basis for music-hall turns. The language game stops as abruptly as it started. There is a short pause as Carr returns to the present and then it is time for another imaginary conversation. This time Tzara is the epitome of Wildean polish: 'Oh, pleasure, pleasure! What else should bring anyone anywhere?' (p. 36). Inconsistency is the only true form of consistency.

Tzara may look and sound like Jack, yet his topics of conversation are remarkably different. He repeats the slogan 'Dada' thirty-four times, not in the strident tones of an artistic revolutionary but in a drawing-room drawl. Carr loses his patience as this scene also slides out of his control and calls Tzara a 'little Rumanian wog' and a 'Balkan turd' (p. 40). Tzara remains dressed as Jack. Ros and Guil were dressed in period costume but spoke and acted in recognizably modern ways. The more complicated structure of *Travesties* allows Stoppard to play several variations on the theme of misleading appearances. Tzara plays both Jack and himself. He attacks 'causality' at the beginning of this scene in keeping with his anti-historical views, although he does so in a manner, and presumably with the mannerisms, appropriate for Wilde:

TZARA: Oh, what nonsense you talk!
CARR: It may be nonsense, but at least it is clever nonsense.

TZARA: I am sick of cleverness. The clever people try to impose a design on the world and when it goes calamitously wrong they call it fate. In point of fact, everything is Chance, including design. (p. 37)

Here and elsewhere Stoppard is sometimes close to the letter of Wilde, for instance, Jack's comment that he is 'sick to death of cleverness' (I.1.630). Much of the writing is, however, in the spirit of Wilde. The potential clash between the Wildean tone and the Dadaist sentiments is held in check here, although such an unlikely balance always proves to be a precarious one.

There is a more submerged conflict present in Carr's own representation of himself. He is occasionally unable to contain his own experiences of the war within the Wildean framework or façade. His fantasies do not always blot out reality. He believes, like Malquist, that the dandy is the true hero:

. . . I had hardly set foot in France before I sank in up to the knees in a pair of twill jodhpurs with pigskin straps handstitched by Ramidge and Hawkes. And so it went on – the sixteen ounce serge, the heavy worsteds, the silk flannel mixture – until I was invalided out with a bullet through the calf of an irreplaceable lambs-wool dyed khaki in the yarn to my own specification. (p. 37)

More realistic notes creep in, however, both during his performance as Algernon and when he is in the present:

– Wonderful spirit in the trenches – never in the whole history of human conflict was there anything to match the courage, the comradeship, the warmth, the cold, the mud, the stench – fear – folly – Christ Jesu! (p. 41)

His front about life at the front momentarily collapses. Like Ros and Guil, he conducts his imaginary conversations to ward off gloomy introspection.

This conflicting reminiscence about life in the trenches occurs after the scene with Tzara has gone off the rails. The subject of the First World War finally shatters the calm of Half Moon Street: drawling gives way to bawling. Carr always gives as good as he gets in these kind of stormy exchanges, which is part of Stoppard's plan to travesty history by allowing a footnote to become part of the main text. Tzara, displaying the Dadaist love of contradiction, puts the case for both economic causation and personal accident. Carr counters with a common sense patriotism. The Wildean tone may get lost but not the costumes.

The basic structure of Wilde's play is retained, despite the stop–go nature of this particular production of it. Tzara, like Jack, leads a double life. He passes himself off at the library as Jack Tzara because he does not want to be recognized as a Dadaist, whereas he is known as Tristan Tzara everywhere else. The cigarette case which gives Jack away in *The Importance* becomes a library ticket in *Travesties*. Tzara is a Rumanian poet who is cast as Jack Worthing who in turn casts himself as Ernest Worthing. Nothing succeeds like excess. This new scene also roller-coasts out of control with the introduction of explicitly ideological questions. Tzara, still dressed as Jack, goes on to chant 'Dada' with its full rhetorical force. Carr is allowed to hold his own not just to make a point about the way in which history ignores the little man, but also because Stoppard sympathizes with his liberal opinions. Stoppard is, however, able to sympathize with most opinions up to the proverbial point. Like Guil and Moon, he can argue both sides against the middle and then take the middle position. He has more in common with Tzara than is generally recognized. Like a Dadaist poem, *Travesties* is a collection of fragments which have been re-arranged to form a new work of art. The side of Dadaism which appeals to Stoppard is the one which emphasizes vitality, playfulness and a cultivated naïvety. Tzara was in many respects a practical joker who teased his readers with contradictions. He wanted to recover the 'innocent pleasure' of both writing and reading. Yet Stoppard's re-arrangement of his fragmentary material is a polished, self-consciously artistic exercise rather than a random one. He therefore parts company with Tzara and joins both Wilde and Joyce. Joyce is caricatured by Carr although, with a nice irony, it is possible to read Carr's narration as an affectionate tribute to Joyce's stream of consciousness techniques. Thus Carr's narration provides another example of the clash between form and content. As suggested, parody is double-voiced in an explicitly ideological way. It also usually contains two voices at a stylistic level. Such a definition fits *Rosencrantz* in which the voices of Shakespeare and Stoppard/Beckett bounce off each other. It is, however, rather inadequate for *Travesties* in which there is a bewildering medley of voices all containing more than an echo of Stoppard's own voice. Perhaps *Travesties* is not just a parody but a parody of parody.

Carr climbs back into the driving seat of his own double-decker entertainment after his row with Tzara. He cues in Joyce and Gwendolen to play Lady Bracknell and her daughter. Joyce is still being cast as a badly dressed stage Irishman: 'the proudest boast of an Irishman is – I paid back my way ...' (p. 50). He wants to borrow money for the English Players' production of *The Importance*. Carr and Tzara have already had a heated debate on the general issue of literary and artistic patronage.

Joyce raises the more specific issue of theatrical patronage. He requires a subsidy from Carr, who is presumably being approached as a member of the British government. *Rosencrantz* deals more fully with relationships between production and patronage, although this self-reflexive debate also becomes a part of the metadrama in *Travesties*. Joyce wins Carr over by playing upon his dandyism and describing *The Importance* almost entirely in terms of Algernon's costumes. Carr agrees to act the part of Algernon as well as that of a patron. Joyce's manipulation of Carr during this scene follows the pattern in which first Bennett and then Tzara steal the show. Just as Ros and Guil remain bewildered attendant lords, so Carr's fantasies ultimately reveal the reality of his subordinate position.

Carr and Joyce exit to discuss arrangements for the production, just as Algernon and Lady Bracknell withdraw to consider the music for her last reception of the season. Tzara now declares his love for Gwendolen. He offers her a hat full of fragments from Shakespeare as well as a definition of the artist as a liar and cheat:

All poetry is a reshuffling of a pack of picture cards, and all poets are cheats. I offer you a Shakespeare sonnet, but it is no longer his. It comes from the wellspring where my atoms are uniquely organised, and my signature is written in the hand of chance. (p. 53)

Tzara seems to imply that writers who reveal that they are liars are, paradoxically, telling a fundamental literary truth. Stoppard appears to tell the truth about lying in *Travesties*! He makes little attempt to disguise the fact that he is reshuffling the literary pack. Such an activity is designed to raise questions about the autonomous nature of any literary text. *Rosencrantz* is based on *Hamlet* which is in its turn based on an earlier play. *Travesties* is based on *The Importance* which is in its turn a parody of some of the dominant themes of Victorian melodrama. *Travesties* also borrows from *Ulysses* which, as Tzara indicates, borrows from 'Homer's *Odyssey* and the Dublin Street Directory for 1904' (p. 44). It is no accident that *Travesties* draws particular attention to the Oxen of the Sun section of *Ulysses*, which both anthologizes and parodies the development of English prose. Perhaps some writer will eventually reshuffle *Travesties* itself and tell a story about wartime Zurich from Bennett's point of view. Stoppard implies that parody should not be dismissed as a lower form of literary life, a parasite that merely feeds off great or popular texts.

Stoppard plays one of Tzara's games by using fragments from a number of Shakespeare's plays as the basis for a discussion of poetry. This Dadaist experiment does not, like the one in the Library, produce uttered nonsense. Tzara's cynicism and Gwendolen's idealism both emerge clearly from the tangle of Shakespearian quotations. These views parallel those of Jack and Gwendolen in *The Importance*: he affects to be a cynical man about town, while she is conscious of living in, and up to, 'an age of ideals' (I.1.392). The poem that Tzara and Gwendolen reconstruct from Shakespeare's sonnet is also not devoid of meaning. A hidden, pornographic script emerges, which forces Gwendolen to change the subject and the idiom. A phrase about the weather allows her to make the switch from Dadaist Shakespeare to Stoppardian Wilde:

Pray don't talk to me about the weather, Mr. Tzara. Whenever people talk to me about the weather I always feel quite certain that they mean something else.

(p. 55)

Such quick changes of idiom become the idiom of *Travesties*. Malquist's belief that it was necessary to 'withdraw with style from the chaos' (p. 21) is reversed. Stoppard creates his own style out of chaotic clashes and oppositions.

Another of these clashes takes place when Joyce interrogates Tzara. The scene parallels the famous one in *The Importance*, except that it is concerned with artistic rather than social credentials. It is done, however, in the interrogatory style which dominates the later sections of *Ulysses*. Yet, just to confuse matters even more, there is also a clash towards the end between Joyce's deadpan style of cross-examination and his flamboyant actions. He pulls out white carnations, silk handkerchiefs and a string of flags from his hat. Anything Tzara can do, he can do better. Tzara, still dressed as Jack Worthing, responds with a heated denunciation of artistic subtlety. Joyce up-stages him again, although this time by dropping the idiom of *Ulysses* in favour of that of *The Importance*:

You are an over-excited little man, with a need for self-expression far beyond the scope of your natural gifts. This is not discreditable. Neither does it make you an artist. (p. 62)

He goes on to argue the case for the artist as magician or conjurer in something approaching his own voice, but reverts to Lady Bracknell's one for his final flourish:

... I would strongly advise you to try and acquire some genius and if possible some subtlety before the season is quite over. Top o' the morning, Mr. Tzara!

(p. 63)

Stoppard clashes Wilde with stage Irish. This particular juxtaposition of idioms is not as chaotic as it might seem to be. Wilde, although very definitely not a stage Irishman, was nevertheless an Irishman who wrote for the stage.

Act Two

Stoppard is usually lying in wait to ambush an audience after the interval. Act Two of *Travesties* begins with an earnest lecture by Cecily on the development of Marxism. Old Carr warns the audience that the idiom of the play will change dramatically after the interval:

... In fact, anybody hanging on just for the cheap comedy of senile confusion might as well go because now I'm on to how I met Lenin and could have changed the course of history ...   (p. 64)

This direct address between actor and spectators is just one of the ways in which *Travesties* draws attention to its own theatricality. The warning, set as it is within the high comedy of Act One, is doomed to go unheeded. The audience also ought to have a strong suspicion that Carr never met Lenin anyway. Stoppard might therefore be bluffing about what will take place after the interval. It would hardly be the first time that he set up expectations only to cheat on them. This time, however, he ambushes the audience by playing it straight.

Cecily's lecture is interrupted by the return of the spectators. As the stage directions indicate, she '*stands patiently at the front of the stage, waiting for the last members of the audience to come in and sit down*' (p. 66). When they are all sitting uncomfortably, she resumes her lecture. She is an unknown quantity, which increases the uncertainty about how to respond to her lecture. She tried to quieten the babble in the library and apparently has a very methodical approach to learning. Order and method turn out to be the appropriate character notes. Stoppard is attempting to pull off at least a three-decker ambush which most critics regard as a failure. First of all, Cecily's lecture provides a striking contrast to the comic clashes which have preceeded it. It sticks unswervingly to a single idiom, which is the theatrically unpromising one of the academic lecture. Unlike George Moore in *Jumpers*, she does not give rise to unintentional verbal and visual comedy. Her flat, matter-of-fact tone becomes a drone. Her cause is also not helped by the way in which she repeats information about wartime Zurich which the audience already knows. Her monotonous, linear narrative offers a very different kind of history lesson from the more colourful representations of the past which have been plucked out of a hat or a mischievous memory. As such, it provides an effective ambush for spectators who want the rattling good show to carry on rattling around its various tracks.

The second part of the ambush concerns the way in which, more specifically, theatrical styles are brought into conflict. A statically delivered lecture was a common feature in European political theatre in the inter-war years. Cecily therefore ambushes the audience by dragging it away from Wilde and plunging it into a version of Socialist Realism. Act Two in general represents a struggle for theatrical space between a high comedy of ideas and a history play of high ideals. Stoppard may, as some critics suggest, be offering a parody of Brechtian epic theatre in the scenes which involve Cecily and the Lenins. Brecht probably is a part of this parody, although Stoppard's version of political theatre seems to be closer to the earlier productions associated with Vsevolod Meyerhold and Erwin Piscator. It is certainly true that Stoppard's mixture of static and declamatory delivery, use of film screens and attempt to render as naturalistically as possible the train which takes Lenin to the Finland Station all contrast very sharply with the theatre of Wilde. This part of the ambush, which heightens the theatricality of *Travesties*, is also effective.

The third, and least successful part of the ambush, relates more specifically to Cecily herself. Wilde's Cecily has no interest in political economy or philanthropy and is generally anti-intellectual. Stoppard therefore produces another of his clashes by making his Cecily an intellectual who is devoted to economic questions, although this is only apparent to spectators who already know *The Importance*. Wilde's Algernon describes Cecily as an English rose. This offers Stoppard the basis for developing the clash of opposites. He represents Cecily as a physically attractive person who holds unattractive views. He appears to believe that an audience might be ambushed by the fact that an attractive girl delivers an earnest academic lecture. It may not be done well, but the spectators are supposed to be surprised and then amused to find it done at all. Although this part of the ambush deserves to fall flat on its boyish face, the rest of it should be treated more sympathetically. Its failure might after all be a measure of its success. Cecily's lecture has already been regarded as a problem in the theatre and, as the stage directions indicate, the solution has been to edit it severely. This fits in with Stoppard's usual practice of teasing rather than alienating an audience. He is not the best person to convict an audience for its lack of radical political and theatrical convictions.

Cecily, the woman preacher, becomes Cecily, the English rose, when Carr arrives at the library. His masquerade as Tzara's decadent younger brother produces another variation on the actor–spectator relationship. He affects to have been a spectator at his own performance in the English Players' production and tells Cecily that the Consul had 'a personal triumph in a most demanding role' (p. 73). He reviews his performance while he is performing once again the part of Algernon. Like both *Rosencrantz* and *Hound*, *Travesties* suggests that spectators, reviewers and actors are interchangeable parts. The metadrama is intensified when Carr and Cecily, performing a version of Wilde, discuss his merits as playwright. This leads to the slanging match which sends this scene off the rails. There is a clash between the play suggested by Carr's blazer and one which contains blazing rows.

The Wildean idiom is not recovered, however, when Carr decides to play the scene again. He and Cecily continue to argue about Marxism. He asserts that Marx misread history, a proposition which is fraught with irony since his own reading of history is idiosyncratic to put it mildly. Cecily does not put her case so mildly. Carr recasts her as a stripper as she and the scene get out of his control. This produces the clash of opposites which is characteristic of *Travesties*: a Wildean heroine takes off her clothes to the contemporary sound of 'The Stripper' while chanting Marxist slogans in the Zurich Public Library. The clash nevertheless illustrates the unpleasant side of Stoppard's pleasant plays. His early plays either ignore women, as happens to all intents and purposes in *Rosencrantz*, or else represent them as little more than stereotypes, as happens in *Jumpers*. This begins with a secretary swinging across the stage doing a strip-tease. Stoppard hopes to tease the heterosexual male spectators by allowing another character to block their view towards the end of the performance. The secretary has no name or dialogue, although she is on stage for much of the play taking notes while George rehearses his lecture. George's wife, the aptly named Dotty, is a glamorous show-business star who becomes a neurotic. Ruth in *Night and Day* is probably the first part in a full-length Stoppard stage play to break some of the stereotypes. His failure to write convincing parts for women unfortunately takes its toll on *Travesties*. As indicated, at least one part of the ambush at the beginning of Act Two fails because of the stereotypes used in it. It is also very surprising to have a parody of *The Importance* which contains such a weak Lady Bracknell, who, as Alan Bennett proves in *Forty Years On* (1968), is usually such a gift to parodists. Stoppard certainly makes things difficult for himself by casting Joyce as Lady Bracknell, but then he usually likes bringing off the impossible.

Cecily loses her Marxism along with her clothes and drags Carr behind the library desk. The library rapidly becomes the setting for the continuation of the history play about Lenin's life and times. Nadya and Lenin, in an undemonstrative style of acting which clashes with the mannered stylization which accompanies the scenes from Wilde, slowly piece the story together with the help of letters. These may just be fragments of history, in much the same way as Tzara's poems are fragments of culture, but they are treated in a reverential rather than cavalier manner. Although Stoppard does not spell it out, letters and diaries in *The Importance* are shown to be works of fiction. Lenin and his wife, by contrast, treat them as documentary evidence. The play with Carr as its hero now has to fight for space with the one which has Lenin as its hero. Actions take place independently but almost simultaneously, as happened in the library scene at the very beginning. The uneasy co-existence of these two plays allows Stoppard to increase the theatricality. The actors from one play become spectators for the other. When Tzara enters, he stands and watches the history play that has now taken possession of the stage. Cecily and Carr poke their heads up from behind the desk to watch what is going on. Similarly, as the stage directions put it, the Lenins '*stop and stare*' (p. 80) at the antics of their rival actors. Lenin, that great scourge of all things infantile, does not like what he sees.

Lenin, in keeping with the traditions of political theatre, delivers a public speech to the audience. Whereas Cecily had offered it as an improving lecture, he treats it to a more emotive piece of rhetoric. Spectators are being given roles to play. They become part of the history which is being presented to them by being cast as a Russian crowd. Lenin argues that artistic freedom, a concept which has significantly been supported in different ways by Tzara, Joyce and Carr, is just a myth:

> ... The freedom of the bourgeois writer, artist or actor is simply disguised dependence on the money-bag, on corruption, on prostitution. Socialist literature and art will be free because the idea of socialism and sympathy with the working people, instead of greed and careerism, will bring ever new forces to its ranks.
>
> (p. 85)

The awkward construction of this speech clashes with the fluency of much of both Stoppard and Wilde's dialogue. Whereas Lenin throws his points at an audience, Wilde's characters almost throw some of their lines away. Lenin dominates the stage physically and rhetorically, whereas *The Importance* is patterned around a number of conversational duets.

Stoppard, that great champion of the infantile, proceeds to show that Lenin, for all his rhetoric about hypocrisy, was still a hypocrite. There is a clash between the public and the private man. It is revealed that he preferred Pushkin to Mayakovsky, Chekhov to Gorky and Beethoven to everyone. The speaker is a liar. For all his parade of revolutionary theory, Lenin's cultural tastes are shown to be almost as conservative as those of Henry Carr. They both like what they know. The documentary format is used to produce evidence to convict rather than aggrandize the hero. Lenin does not listen to music any more because it makes him want to behave in a friendly way:

> ... Nowadays we can't pat heads or we'll get our hands bitten off. We've got to *hit* heads, hit them without mercy, though ideally we're against doing violence to people ... Hm, one's duty is infernally hard ... (p. 89)

Stoppard finds the rope and Lenin all but hangs himself with it.

Lenin's suppressed love for classical music allows Stoppard to add a musical clash to the wide variety of verbal and visual ones. As the stage directions indicate, Lenin's favourite Beethoven sonata '*degenerates absurdly*' (p. 89) into a music-hall song known as 'Mr Gallagher and Mr Shean'. This was popularized by the American double-act of Ed Gallagher and Al Shean during the Ziegfeld Follies of 1922. It becomes the framing device for the scene from Wilde in which Cecily and Gwendolen meet each other for the first time. Wilde himself indicates that this scene ought to be played in a stylized way with rhythm and to some extent rhyme being more important than naturalistic conversation. Cecily, for instance, introduces herself to Gwendolen with a rhyming couplet: 'Pray let me introduce myself to you. My name is Cecily Cardew' (II.2.565–6). As so often, Stoppard turns Wilde's understatement into overstatement:

CECILY: Oh dear Miss Carr, oh dear Miss Carr,
          pleasure remain exactly where you are –
          I beg you don't get up –
GWEN: I think we'll need another cup –
          Pray sit down, Miss Carruthers,
CECILY: So kind of you, Miss Carr. (p. 90)

Form and content are brought, once again, into opposition: an American music-hall turn which is associated with a male double-act forms the basis for a scene in which two Victorian ladies have tea. As happens in Wilde, the façade of politeness cracks under the weight of partial revelations about the double identities of both Jack and Algernon. Stoppard overstates Wilde again by clashing mannered manners with contemporary expletives. Cecily's response to the news that both she and Gwendolen are apparently in love with a Tristan Tzara is 'And up yours, Miss Carr' (p. 93). The Victorian costumes, like the Elizabethan ones in *Rosencrantz*, suggest one play, whereas the language suggests another.

The scene is now set for recognitions and reconciliations. Resolutions have never been Stoppard's smartest suit. When he does offer them, as in *Hound*, it is a parody of neat denouements. This also happens at the end of *Travesties*. The denouement of *The Importance* is, in keeping with the rest of the play, an artificial and contrived one. Stoppard sets out to parody what is in itself a parody of the melodramatic and sentimental denouements associated with the Victorian theatre. He does this by quickening the pace. The recognitions and reconciliations at the end of *Travesties* need to be played at break-neck speed. Although not even Wilde can find a solution as to how Algernon might become Ernest, Stoppard comes up with an unlikely answer. This is related to some complicated stage business about fragments of writing which have been misplaced. To explain precisely what happens here would be to lose sight of the fact that everything is meant to appear unlikely. It is, however, appropriate that chapters from books, rather than babies, go astray in a play which is such a self-conscious piece of writing about writing. It is wildly inappropriate, and therefore totally appropriate for *Travesties*, for James Joyce to boom out a variation on one of Lady Bracknell's famous lines: 'Miss Carr, where is the missing chapter???' (p. 97).

The metadrama is increased by the way in which Bennett summarizes the reviews of Carr's performance in the role of Algernon. Just to confuse the confusion, it seems that Carr's memory has jumped the rails and that he is playing the first scene while everybody else is doing the last one:

The *Neue Zuricher Zeitung* and the *Zuricher Post* announce respectively the cultural high and low point of the theatrical season at the Theater zur Kaufleuten yesterday evening. The *Zeitung* singles you out for a personal triumph in a demanding role. (p. 95)

Actors, patrons, reviewers and spectators are all interchangeable parts in *Travesties*.

The Importance ends with a courtship ritual which parodies Shakespeare's festive comedies as well as Victorian drama. The pairs of lovers embrace each other in a patterned, stylized manner. Stoppard overstates this by turning it into a '*formal, short dance sequence*' (p. 97), which clashes with Cecily and Gwendolen's earlier song and dance act. As Stoppard says in the stage directions, this formal dance represents '*a complete dislocation of the play*' (p. 97). He ends a play which has been concerned throughout with dislocations, notably between form and content, by dislocating some of the previous dislocations. A formal period dance closes a play which has been anything but formal and historically authentic.

Carr, the literary footnote, has the last word. He and Cecily appear on stage as an elderly married couple. Cecily is still pedantic and methodological. She pulls the rug out from underneath her husband by confirming that he never knew Lenin. His dilemma about whether he could have prevented the Russian Revolution has been a delusion of grandeur, as has been the casting of the real consul as his butler. Yet 'Carr of the Consulate' refuses to be put off by such trivial considerations as the truth. He is still engaged in the serious business of reshuffling the pack of lies which he palms off as his memories.

Stoppard and Fellini

Federico Fellini once declared that the act of memory was like watching 'a dozen films simultaneously'. This is certainly the impression that is conveyed by his film *8½* (1963). Like Stoppard's plays, it holds its mirror up to itself and artistic processes in general. A film director, Guido Anselmi, is unenthusiastic about a box-office film which he has been contracted to direct. He wants, instead, to shoot a film of his own life. To over-simplify, *8½* contains one film, which chronicles the attempt to get the box-office spectacular off the ground, and another one in which Guido self-consciously directs scenes from his life. The movement of the film therefore resembles the jumpy, bumpy ride of *Travesties* along its various tracks. As with Carr's narration, there is always doubt about whether Guido is directing 'real' or 'imaginary' scenes, or a mixture of the two. He appears to retreat from the real, as represented by a film script about a holocaust which demands a series of decisions he is unable to make, into a more private world in which he shapes, and to some extent controls, his life by framing it within cinematic images. Fellini suggests that films themselves, like the directors who make them, will collapse with nervous exhaustion unless they retain a belief in the liberating power of illusion and magic. Films can only be true to themselves if they tell lies. Like Stoppard, Fellini finds the magic and illusion which a film has to try to recapture within childhood itself, or else in locations like the circus ring which conjure up childhood. Carr's narration is significantly the product of senility or second childhood. The film that Guido is supposed to be making is a 'disaster movie', which spells disaster for the spirit if not the finances of the film industry because it denies a set of subjective explorations and responses. Lenin fulfils some of the functions of this 'disaster movie' in *Travesties*. As represented by Stoppard, he stands for large projects which demand a series of decisions that invariably suppress and repress the subjective in favour of the objective.

8½, like Stoppard's plays, constantly reviews itself, perhaps most obviously through the running commentary of the script-writer. It holds a mirror up to itself by showing what is involved in the pre-production of a film: casting, haggling with producers and agents, arguing with script-writers and assistants, supervising the construction of a set and carrying out screen tests. This artistic turmoil is paralleled by a more personal one. The scene in which Guido plays back the screen tests for Pace, the producer, may be related to Stoppard's use of plays within plays in *Rosencrantz*. It takes place in a large cinema auditorium, although there are only a handful of spectators for the screening. They include Guido's wife, Luisa. Guido has in fact been screen testing for the film about his life, so she sees a representation of herself. It is both unmistakably her, while at the same time also being one of the actresses who plays her. Fellini flips the same double-sided coins as Stoppard does: actor–spectator, performer–patron and rehearsal–performance. Guido is forced by Pace to give a press conference on the set for the box-office film. The journalists want him, and therefore his film, to make immediate, quotable statements. They end up taunting him, and Fellini's film, for having 'nothing to say'. The film therefore offers a parodic review of itself. Journalists and academics have often accused Stoppard of having 'nothing to say', even though they usually concede that he says it very well. *Travesties*, like *8½*, does not lend itself to labels and slogans. They both appear to be affirming, in their different but nevertheless overlapping ways, that art can only be true to itself. Both works appear to tell the truth about lying.

Postmodernism

This brief comparison between *Travesties* and *8½* is not meant to suggest that Stoppard was directly influenced by Fellini, or indeed by any other 'new wave' film directors. It is designed, rather, to establish two related points. First of all, it provides another illustration of the fact that films, television and radio programmes often provide the best contexts for an appreciation of Stoppard's works. Much has been written recently about the 'cine novel', not enough about 'cine drama'. The second, and more important point, concerns Stoppard's relationship with new artistic waves. Although it would be inaccurate to describe *8½* as a postmodernist film, it is nevertheless one which anticipates many of the artistic positions now associated with postmodernism. Fellini therefore has a reputation for innovation which is often denied to Stoppard. This obviously has something to do with the fact that *8½* was made over ten years before the first production of *Travesties*. It is not, however, quite so simple. Theories of postmodernism have tended to confine themselves to fiction and film, as well as to architecture and the visual arts, to the exclusion of drama. This emphasis often reflects the artistic preoccupations and practices of the leading theoreticians themselves. Alain Robbe-Grillet, for instance, produces novels and film scripts, alongside his theoretical writings, rather than plays. It is probably true that this kind of concentration has worked against an appreciation of Stoppard as an innovative and self-consciously contemporary writer. It is certainly true that the few critics who approach his work within the context of postmodernism are among his strongest supporters. Ronald Hayman's reading of Stoppard within the context of 'anti-theatre' provides a good illustration of this set of connections.

Postmodernism is associated with a number of practices, which will already be quite familiar as a result of this particular reading of some of Stoppard's works. It denies the credibility of privileged, omniscient narration, especially when it offers credible explanations for motives and actions. The narrator may or may not know the truth about someone or something. He or she may or may not choose to reveal what appears to be true. Postmodernist writers tend to represent character not in terms of a psychologically convincing and explicable inner core, but rather in terms of series of surfaces or 'instant characters'. Such surfaces, representing as they do the chaos of both presentation and reception of self, are meant to be inconsistent. Character is defined, insofar as it is capable of definition at all, through such inconsistencies. Postmodernist texts often represent the divisions and fractures associated with schizophrenia. Stoppard also does this, in an admittedly gentle and jokey way, through Carr's narration in *Travesties* and, to a lesser extent, through the attendant lords' problems over identity in *Rosencrantz*. Some theorists, perhaps most notably Frederic Jameson, have suggested that post-modernism itself is the product of cultural schizophrenia. Its writings, like the society in which they are produced and consumed, are split between an affirmation of the contemporary and a denial of it.

Postmodernist texts are self-consciously structured around gaps, silences and absences rather than around a definable and knowable body of information. Narratives are constantly broken off or interrupted never to be resumed. There is no last word. This process is often trans-lated into a game with the reader or spectator. The absence of an omniscient narrator necessitates the active presence of the reader or spectator. This heightened awareness of the reception, or consumption, of literature leads to a dominant emphasis on voyeurism. It is often both the theme of the narrative and the form of its narration. This in turn leads to obsessions with pornography by male writers such as John Hawkes and Robbe-Grillet himself. Jameson's analysis poses the ques-tion of whether these concerns with consumption, voyeurism and pornography represent a critique of consumerism or an often disturbing celebration of it. Voyeurism is one of Stoppard's major themes in *Rosen-crantz*. The Player asserts the position, familiar in postmodernist writ-ings, that a text is defined by its readers or spectators. They are the authors of it. Stoppard also flirts with pornographic representations in *Rosencrantz*, *Malquist* and *Travesties*, although these are relatively tame in comparison with the more sadistic ones on offer.

Parody and voyeurism often function as different sides of the same coin. Readers are given glimpses of known and knowable texts such as detective stories, only to discover that what they consider to be vital clues or scenes are withheld completely from them. The familiar, which involves passive reception, becomes the unfamiliar, which involves active reception. As noticed earlier during the discussion of Linda Hutcheon's argument, parody celebrates and therefore reinforces the cultural legacy of the past, while at the same time seeking to deny it and emancipate readers from it. Perhaps this too is an example of cultural schizophrenia. Jameson's position is rather different from Hutcheon's one in that he sees pastiche, rather than parody, as being a distinctive feature of post-modernism. He regards parody as part of a conscious art of authorship, whereas pastiche is taken to represent a more neutral form of 'mimicry'. His conclusions are not as important or as accurate as the way in which he frames the original questions. He draws attention to the way in which postmodernist writers have been fascinated precisely by that whole landscape of advertising and motels, of the Las Vegas strip, of the late show and Grade-B Hollywood film, of so-called paraliterature with its airport paperback categories of the gothic and the romance, the popular biography, the murder mystery and the science fiction or fantasy novel.

He goes on to suggest that postmodernists do not just quote from such popular texts, but use them at a much more fundamental level as the basis for their own writings. This is seen as calling into question traditional distinctions between high and popular culture, as well as posing more fundamental questions about the ownership of these cultures. Answers are bound to differ, particularly when given within the context of a general discussion. My own impressions are not of a neutral pastiche but rather of an aesthetic which, while not being necessarily explicitly camp, nevertheless offers a good taste of bad taste. It can still be established with some confidence that Stoppard poses many of the same questions as both the theoreticians and practitioners of postmodernism do. Both *Rosencrantz* and *Travesties* are sustained explorations of ones relating to differences between high and popular cultures and the role of the spectator within them.

Postmodernism usually only allows readers or spectators to identify with themselves. The rules of the game prevent, say, links between them and a tragic character such as Hamlet. This tends to produce a tone that is broadly comic, although this can take gothic, grotesque or truly absurdist forms which are very different from the more jaunty ones adopted by Stoppard. Although obviously difficult to generalize, this in turn often reinforces a lack of explicit engagement with and commitment to political causes. A necessarily fragmented text may say things about itself, but is unable to offer coherent and omniscient guidelines. It seeks to challenge the validity of such guidelines and in particular the public language in which they are framed. This language itself is held to be a fictitious one and is opposed by competing, fragmentary, private languages. *Rosencrantz* offers a fairly basic variation on this theme by contrasting the public language of the Danish court with Ros and Guil's more private one. As emphasized, it also refuses to engage with political issues. This is not the kind of disengagement that is often to be found in romantic and modernist writings, caused by cultural pessimism. Such pessimism presupposes a vision either of how society was in the past, or how it ought to be in the present and future. Again it is difficult to generalize, but much postmodernist writing lacks an explicitly political and social vision.

Such a sketchy survey of what is by its own definitions a sketchy subject is bound to be rather an inadequate one. It should nevertheless at least suggest that there are some grounds for claiming that Stoppard is a postmodernist writer. This proposition still has to be hedged around with qualifications. Some of these have already been indicated. Other ones might include the fact that Stoppard's cult of childhood is an essentially romantic concept. It also needs to be stressed again that Joyce, the author who represents the magic and mystery of the artist, is given something approaching the last word in *Travesties*. Although the structures of both *Travesties* and *Rosencrantz* appear to be fragmentary ones, they are nevertheless still examples of the well-made, self-consciously authored play. This might suggest that, while Stoppard may flirt with versions of postmodernism, he is unable to commit himself to them. He writes about writing but wants to retain his own privileged position as a writer. The question then has to be asked about what kind of writer he is. This is one to which reviewers and critics tend to give rather confused answers. The debate is about whether he is a 'serious artist' or a show-business 'siren'. His work can, quite legitimately, be compared with Fellini's complex analysis of films and filming and Mel Brooks's screwball comedies. This certainly represents a problem, although the real one is the way in which the original questions are framed. It is, for instance, taken as read that there is a polarity between the 'artist' and the 'siren'. Stoppard himself tends to give credence to this position by accepting its categories, while at the some time reserving the right to leap-frog between them. As indicated earlier on, Susan Sontag's analysis of camp suggests that the polarity between the two positions may be a misleading one. The serious artist can only remain one in mass, consumer society by becoming a show-business siren. He or she covers the cultural waterfront in an attempt to construct a good taste of bad taste. This is the essential point to establish about Stoppard and his particular brand of camp theatre. It must, however, remain more of an open question as to whether this position can be related to the dominant assumptions behind postmodernist writing. An admittedly tentative answer might be that, despite some of the important qualifications, there is still a case for locating Stoppard within this movement. *Travesties* in particular needs to be seen as an innovative contribution to contemporary obsessions with parody in particular and writing about writing in general.

7. Shakespeare Revisited

Introduction

Stoppard suggests in his Preface to *Dogg's Hamlet, Cahoot's Macbeth* that these two quite distinct plays form a unified whole. He points out that 'the first is hardly a play at all without the second, which cannot be performed without the first' (p. 7). *Dogg's Hamlet* grew out of two shorter pieces which Stoppard wrote for Ed Berman, alias Professor R. L. Dogg, and his community-based theatre projects. *Dogg's Our Pet*, which was first performed at Berman's Almost Free Theatre in Soho in 1971, was a sketch based around Ludwig Wittgenstein's concept of language games. Stoppard originally constructed *The (15 Minute) Dogg's Troupe Hamlet* for Berman's touring playbus, although it was first performed as a platform sketch at the National Theatre in 1976. It provided a trailer or warm-up for the National's own production of *Hamlet*. *Cahoot's Macbeth*, as Stoppard explains in the Preface, arose out of his increasing concern with the plight of Czechoslovakian dissidents. He returned in 1977 to the country of his birth and met writers, actors and others who had fallen foul of the new authorities. An actor called Pavel Kahout later wrote to tell him about 'Living Room Theatre':

What is L R T? A call-group. Everybody, who wants to have Macbeth at home with two great and forbidden Czech actors, Pavel Landovsky and Vlasta Chramostova, can invite his friends and call us. Five people will come with one suitcase' (p. 8)

Dogg's Hamlet, Cahoot's Macbeth, which was first performed in 1979, belongs to the period when Stoppard's work became more explicitly political. It may therefore be related to *Every Good Boy Deserves Favour* (1977) and *Professional Foul*. The material that goes to make up *Dogg's Hamlet*, however, belongs to the period when Stoppard was committed about being uncommitted. Taken together, then, these two interrelated plays dramatize very effectively Stoppard's theatrical development during the 1970s. It must nevertheless remain an open question as to whether *Dogg's Hamlet, Cahoot's Macbeth* forms a unified whole.

Dogg's Hamlet

Dogg's Hamlet is set at a boys' preparatory school which is preparing for a speech day. The immediate ambush for the audience is that the very

126

obviously English schoolboys nevertheless speak a language known as Dogg. This sounds like school slang at times, although it is in fact a language in its own right. It consists of familiar enough English words whose meanings are now either altered or, in many cases, completely reversed. For example, 'useless, git' in Dogg means 'afternoon, sir', whereas 'afternoon, squire' means 'get stuffed, you bastard'. Wittgenstein referred to language as a maze in his *Philosophical Investigations* (1963 edn), which is Stoppard's main source of inspiration:

Language is a labyrinth of paths. You approach from *one* side and know your way about; you approach the same place from the other side and no longer know your way about.

Stoppard only wants to tease rather than alienate members of the audience, so he provides them with clues as to how to get out of this maze by learning Dogg. Significantly, adults are being taught how to speak by children. The easiest words to pick up are those which are defined either through their associations with various stage props, for instance the microphone, or else through on-stage reactions to them. This process is referred to by Wittgenstein and others as the 'ostensive teaching of words'. Mr Dogg, the Headmaster, responds to the question 'cretinous pig-faced, git?' (p. 16) by looking at his watch.

Easy, a lorry driver from Leamington Spa, arrives with building materials to construct a stage for the school play. Like the audience, he starts off by not having any clues about Dogg. He greets the Headmaster with a cheery 'Afternoon, squire' (p. 20) and then forms a human chain to get everything off his lorry, which is known in Dogg as an 'artichoke' (p. 19). The two languages are sometimes not that far apart, although far enough when it comes to building materials. To take just one example, 'slab' means 'okay' in Dogg. Easy shouts 'slab' a couple of times and gets what he wants, but then he and the audience are ambushed when the coincidence no longer holds. This pattern continues throughout the building of the platform or stage. The construction of this platform is obviously a metaphor for the construction of language. Critics become so wrapped up in the philosophical and linguistic games that are going on here that they fail to notice that Easy, occasionally unwittingly aided by the schoolboys, is building a stage on a stage. *Dogg's Hamlet*, as will become even more apparent later on, needs to be seen as another of Stoppard's self-conscious pieces of metadrama.

The stage is eventually set for speeches and a production of *Hamlet*. A Lady enters and addresses the on-stage audience. Her speech, which in

Dogg, is all about healthy little bodies and minds, means something very different in English. Dogg is often the reverse side of the coin from English:

... Sad facts, brats pule puke crap-pot stink, spit; grow up dunces crooks; rank socks dank snotrags, conkers, ticks; crib books, cock snooks, block bogs, jack off, catch pox pick spots, scabs, padlocks, seek kicks, kinks, slack; nick swag, swig coke, bank kickbacks; ... frankly can't stick kids ...   (p. 28)

If this is received as English, then there is the kind of comic clash of form and content which dominates *Travesties*. The Lady's gracious tone is entirely inappropriate for her subject matter. Everything is upside down at this speech day. Fox Major, who wins all the prizes including the one for 'pelvic wiggle stamp' (p. 29), takes the table rather than the various trophies on it.

Easy is the theatre audience's representative when he first appears. Yet he picks up, or catches, Dogg quite quickly. Wittgenstein specifically refers to 'cursing' as a language game. Easy joins in with the schoolboys who are swearing at Mr Dogg because he has ordered the stage to be re-built yet again. He also announces the title of the play in Dogg: 'Hamlet bedsocks Denmark. Yeti William Shakespeare' (p. 31). Critical opinion differs about the effect of the introduction of Shakespearian English. It can be argued that it achieves a new freshness and accessibility by being set alongside the confusions of Dogg. If you are trapped in a linguistic maze, then the sound of Shakespeare genuinely becomes music to the ears. If this is correct, then Stoppard is reversing the treatment of Elizabethan language in *Rosencrantz*, in which the text of *Hamlet* becomes confusing, not just because it is severely edited but also because it is framed by idiomatic, conversational English. The problem with such an interpretation of *Dogg's Hamlet* is not, of course, that it makes Stoppard inconsistent. He has always been more than happy to reverse positions and coins. It is, rather, that Shakespeare's words are being spoken by actors who do not have a clue about what they mean. Dogg-speakers are now being thrown into the linguistic maze. The assumption must be that their inflection and emphasis are all over the place. An early warning of this comes when the schoolboys rehearse their parts before the arrival of Easy. They have conned them by rote without understanding a single word. Stoppard may therefore be setting up expectations of familiarity among his audience but, as is his wont, not necessarily fulfilling them. If nothing else, the speed of this production of *Hamlet* should warn against seeing it as representing the familiar in unfamiliar surroundings.

Members of the on-stage audience for the Lady's speech now become actors in *Hamlet*. Theatricality is increased by the presence of an on-stage audience for the play. The Lady becomes a spectator instead of an actress. She should be joined by Mr Dogg, after he has delivered the Prologue, Easy and a token number of boys. On-stage reactions to the play are part of the spectacle for the theatre audience. Like *Hound*, *Dogg's Hamlet* shows its audience a reflection of itself. Both plays also parody production techniques. Although the schoolboy actors wear costumes that pass for Elizabethan ones, their school uniform is meant to be clearly visible underneath. Ophelia, who is played by a boy called Charlie, should be instantly recognizable as a schoolboy. Gertrude is played in matronly style by Mrs Dogg, who is probably more worried by the dirt behind Hamlet's, or Fox Major's, ears than by his 'antic disposition'. Alan Bennett offers a more extended parody of the school play in *Forty Years On*. Stoppard's parody returns to some of the themes of *Rosencrantz*. As indicated, the theatre is shown to be unable to reproduce nature, more particularly the weather. This is part of a wider argument which reveals, but also revels in, artifice and theatricality. *Dogg's Hamlet* continues the argument. This production of *Hamlet* boasts '*a cut-out sun, moon and crown*' (p. 31) which, with a bit of luck, can be swung into position at the appropriate moment:

FRANCISCO: But look, the morn in russet mantle clad
            Walks o'er the dew of yon high eastern hill.
            (*On 'But look' a cut-out sun shoots up over the stage left screen,
            and descends here.*)   (p. 32)

Although a lot of expense has been spared on the production, no energy is spared when it comes to sound effects. Hamlet and Horatio appear on the battlements at Elsinore to the accompaniment of '*Noise of carouse, cannon, fireworks*' (p. 33), which probably means that the cymbals are working overtime. This is immediately replaced by '*Wind noise*' (p. 33) for the Ghost. Scenes involving the court are accompanied by a '*Flourish of trumpets*' (p. 34). The more private, domestic setting of the closet scene is suggested by '*Lute music*' (p. 36). Stoppard also returns to the sound effects which he parodied so successfully in *Rosencrantz*, namely those associated with theatrical life on the ocean wave:

At sea.
Sea music. A sail appears above stage left screen. Enter HAMLET *on platform, swaying as if on ship's bridge. He wipes his eyes, and becomes seasick. End sea music. Exit* HAMLET, *holding his hand to his mouth.*   (p.37)

The inclusion of this scene, which is Stoppard's rather than Shakespeare's, makes a nonsense of the claims that are sometimes made that *Dogg's Hamlet* is only offering a radically edited version of Shakespeare. As the whole show has to be done in about thirteen minutes flat, it means that nobody has time to attend to attendant lords like Rosencrantz and Guildenstern who do not make an appearance. The coarse acting of the schoolboys, together with these creaking props and sound effects, makes a dog's dinner of *Hamlet*.

A thirteen-minute version of *Hamlet* is too easy for Stoppard. He plays the mischievous projectionist again, this time speeding up the reel rather than cutting between different ones. The whole idea of a two-minute encore to *Hamlet* is absurd in itself. The performance falls completely apart at the seams: the sound effects merge into one another and the '*cut-out sun, moon and crown*' flaps around with bewildering rapidity. Lines are delivered to the wrong characters and there are, presumably, a number of collisions on stage as the actors make their hasty entrances and exits. The corpses leap to their feet and take a bow at the end of both Stoppard's shortened versions: now they are dead, now they are not. Now you see it, now you don't.

Cahoot's Macbeth

Stoppard's ambushes often depend on an audience being lulled into a false sense of security. *Dogg's Hamlet* certainly teases the spectators, particularly during the first few minutes As the play goes on, however, the maze can become quite a secure and enjoyable place. First of all, it should prove relatively easy to pick up a smattering of Dogg, just as Easy does. Secondly, sophisticated adults are given the opportunity to laugh at the coarse acting of schoolboys. Thirdly, the sense of security that the spectators achieve through acting out this patronizing role can be enhanced if they are familiar with the kind of school productions that are being parodied. As suggested, *Travesties* changes its spots while the interval is in progress: the comic climate of the first part is replaced by a very literal emphasis on the importance of being earnest. A broadly similar change occurs between the two parts of *Dogg's Hamlet, Cahoot's Macbeth*. The second part begins, not with actors rehearsing their lines or a stage being constructed, but with the performance of Shakespeare itself. Stoppard teases the audience by holding back the framing device for this particular production. Those spectators who know the text of *Macbeth* reasonably well will notice that this version of it is an edited one. This is a familiar way of doing the play: emphasizing its thriller-like pace at the expense of establishing either general atmosphere or particular characters such as Duncan. The text is edited and the staging almost certainly suffers from under-rehearsal. These were comic devices in *Dogg's Hamlet*. Stoppard offers his own version of the thriller by keeping his spectators in suspense. To laugh or not to laugh? That is the question that he poses at the beginning of *Cahoot's Macbeth*.

Stoppard keeps the suspense going by only imparting a bit of information at a time. After the witches have melted into the air, the stage lights go up to reveal that the performance is taking place in a living-room. This is a potentially comic revelation, since domestic interiors and blasted heaths do not appear to have that much in common. The schoolboy actors in *Dogg's Hamlet* drew attention to the artificiality of performance through both their costumes and their comically absurd naturalistic devices. The setting of *Macbeth*, with its panoramic sweep of sea shores, heaths, castles and forests, within the confines of a domestic interior represents a different kind of ambush of naturalistic conventions and expectations. Even though the framing device is slowly revealed, any laughter at the clash between staging and content must remain somewhat uneasy.

Stoppard enjoys making an audience wait. He finally interrupts the performance after the murder of Duncan, which takes place well into the second act of Shakespeare's play. A police siren is heard while Lady Macbeth delivers the line 'I heard the owl scream and the crickets cry' (p. 52). The Inspector who calls is therefore being associated with the forces of darkness in general and the 'fatal bellman' (II.2.3) in particular. His knocking at the door coincides neatly with the moment in *Macbeth* when MacDuff and Lennox knock on the castle gates. They are eventually admitted by the Porter, who provides the comic relief. The Inspector is thus associated with both the sinister and the comic. He is also a policeman who arrives just after a murder has been committed, which allows Stoppard to play another variation on his parodies of the whodunit. The schoolboys in *Dogg's Hamlet* test the microphone that is going to be used for speech day: 'Breakfast, breakfast ... sun–dock–trog' (p. 15). The Inspector goes through exactly the same routine – 'Testing, testing ... one–two–three ...' (p. 53), although for entirely different reasons. He is checking to make sure that the living-room is bugged, whereas the schoolboys were preparing for a festive occasion. He wants to prevent play and plays, whereas they indulge in them. Such particular correspondences between the actions, if not the motives, in the two plays suggest that it makes sense to see them as different sides of the same coin. Although the Inspector represents the forces of evil, his manner is that of a music-hall comedian: 'is it the National Academy of Dramatic Art, or, as we say down Mexico way, NADA?' (p. 53). This particular copper is menacing on one side and jovial on the other.

Ros and Guil used their clichés as talismans to ward off the confusion caused by the Danish court. This position is reversed in *Cahoot's Macbeth*. The Inspector's clichés carry confusion and worse, while the Shakespearian language carries both comfort and hope. Although the Inspector's patter is made up of a variety of colloquialisms, he has a specialized line in theatrical ones. Ironically, he speaks, or gushes, in a highly theatrical idiom which the actors themselves refuse to use. The spectator is more stagey than the actors:

INSPECTOR: ... I'm a great admirer of yours, you know. I've followed your
   career for years.
'MACBETH':   I haven't worked for years.
INSPECTOR: What are you talking about? – I saw you last season – my wife
   was with me ...
'MACBETH':   It couldn't have been me.
INSPECTOR: It *was* you – you looked great – sounded great – where were
   you last year?
'MACBETH':   I was selling papers in –
INSPECTOR: – the newspaper kiosk at the tram terminus, and you were wonderful! I said to my wife, that's Landovsky – the actor – isn't he great?! What a
   character! Wonderful voice! 'Getcha paper!' – up from here (*he thumps his
   chest.*) – no strain, every syllable given its value ...   (p.54)

The Inspector, playing the part of a stage-struck spectator, does not let his supposed hero get a word in edgeways. He then turns his attention to Lady Macbeth, who has had to work as a waitress because she too is not regarded as politically acceptable:

... I mean, it gives one pause, doesn't it? 'Tonight Macbeth will be played by Mr
Landovsky who last season scored a personal success in the newspaper kiosk at
the tram terminus and has recently been seen washing the floors in number three
boiler factory. The role of Lady Macbeth is in the capable hands of Vera from
The Dirty Spoon' ...   (p. 55)

Stoppard suggests that totalitarianism is a form of over-acting. The Inspector attempts to steal the show, metaphorically as well as literally. The other actors become merely knives and forks to feed him the lines. *Travesties* notices Lenin's dislike of over-acting, although the reference is ironic since he is one of the worst offenders. Despite Stoppard's dislike of Brecht, the representation of totalitarianism in *Cahoot's Macbeth* has some similarities with that in *The Resistable Rise of Arturo Ui* (1941).

The Inspector orders the performance of *Macbeth* to start again and very self-consciously takes up his position as a member of the audience. The actors are reluctant to carry on under this kind of scrutiny, but are bullied into doing so by the Inspector's menacing clichés:

> ... I'm the cream in your coffee, the sugar in your tank, and the breeze blowing down your neck. So let's have a little of the old trouper spirit, because if I walk out of this show I take it with me.   (p. 56)

Given this warning, the spectacle when the play resumes is the spectator. He watches the events surrounding the aftermath of Duncan's murder, culminating in Macduff's announcement that Macbeth has gone to Scone to be invested as the new king. Stoppard is quite prepared to wait for a good pay-off line. This secret policeman believes that the play is over with the crowning of a murderer: 'Very good. Very good! And so nice to have a play with a happy ending for a change' (p. 58). Normalization is his word for usurpation.

Cahoot's Macbeth continues Stoppard's examination of relationships between actors and spectators. The Hostess emerges from the theatre audience to confront the Inspector, when he is checking both his surveillance equipment and comic patter. She claims the right to speak on behalf of the audience, or public. So does the Inspector, although it is quite obvious that he holds this particular one in contempt:

> Don't you find it rather inconvenient, having a lot of preening exhibitionists projecting their voices around the place? – and that's just the audience. I mean, who wants to be packed out night after night by a crowd of fashionable bronchitics saying 'I don't think it's as good as his last one', and expecting to use your lavatory at will?   (p. 53)

He is keen to make sure that nobody leaves before his own performance is over. The spectators are warned not to 'leave the building. You may use the lavatory but leave the door open' (p. 58). The Inspector then proceeds to inspect the audience. Boris and Maurice, his stupid henchmen, have managed to compile a list of who is present. He shines his torch at the audience while reading this out:

> ... Three stokers, two labourers, a van-driver's mate, janitors, street cleaners, a jobbing gardener, painter and decorator, chambermaid, two waiters, farmhand ... you seem to have cracked the problem of the working-class audience ...
>
> (p. 59)

133

The Hostess insists on classifying the spectators by their occupations before normalization. This is a more sinister language game than those that were played in *Dogg's Hamlet.* As the Inspector puts it earlier on: 'Words can be your friend or your enemy, depending on who's throwing the book, so watch your language' (p. 59). He watches the spectators and they in turn have to watch him perform verbal gymnastics.

The Inspector then turns his spotlight away from the audience back onto the actors. Like the Player in *Rosencrantz,* he is always acting in a very stagey manner. The members of the *Macbeth* cast, by contrast, maintain a sharp distinction between themselves and their roles. Ironically, it is Landovsky, the actor who plays Macbeth, who tries to interrupt the Inspector's music-hall turn with references to the constitution. His matter-of-fact statements contrast with the Inspector's more metaphoric responses:

. . . The way I see it, life is lived off the record. It's altogether too human for the written word, it happens in pictures . . . metaphors . . . A few years ago you suddenly had it on toast, but when they gave you an inch you overplayed your hand and rocked the boat so they pulled the rug from under you, and now you're in the doghouse . . . I mean, that is pure fact. Metaphorically speaking . . .

(p. 61)

Ros and Guil's private language has now become part of the official and officious language. The contrast between idiomatic and Shakespearian language, which was at the heart of *Rosencrantz,* is being represented as an irrelevant one in this totalitarian context. As both can be understood by the authorities, so both are capable of appropriation and manipulation. As will become apparent, this means that Dogg language becomes the only way of throwing the book back at the Inspector.

The Inspector's exit unwittingly provides a cue for the performance of *Macbeth* to start again. Shakespeare's play, which deals with the usurpation of legitimate authority, has always offered a general comment on the persecution of actors and audiences in Czechoslovakia. The parallels become more explicit with the arrival of the Inspector. For instance, Macbeth briefs two murderers to kill Banquo. The audience should have no trouble making connections between this scene and the activities of the Inspector, Boris and Maurice. Stoppard edits Shakespeare's text, but retains a number of lines which reinforce the parallels. Macbeth declares that he must, for a time anyway, disguise his 'bare-faced power' (p. 64). He must, like Claudius in *Hamlet,* play the king rather than the murderer. The Inspector is also disguising his own 'bare-faced power' by playing the king of comedy as well as a tyrant.

Easy provides the most important link between *Dogg's Hamlet* and *Cahoot's Macbeth*. He arrives in his 'artichoke' from Leamington Spa with a load of wood. He is now a fluent speaker of Dogg. Stoppard makes this unlikely appearance part of one of his more caviar jokes. Shakespeare's two murderers are baffled by the appearance of a third one, who has not been briefed by Macbeth in their presence. Some of this bewilderment has rubbed off on Shakespearian editors, who are unable to come up with good explanations for the unexpected appearance of a third murderer. Easy wanders on to the living-room stage and finds himself cast in this part. He has, like the Inspector, interrupted the performance, although he allows himself to be escorted off the stage by the Hostess. He makes no attempt to steal the show. Easy the spectator nevertheless unwittingly becomes Easy the actor again when, presumably on his way to check his lorry, he appears on cue as Banquo's ghost. This corresponds to the moment in *Dogg's Hamlet* when the schoolboys cast him briefly as the Ghost of Hamlet's father. He is in both cases being associated with victims of tyranny who nevertheless are instrumental in its overthrow. The fact that Easy arrives from England reinforces such associations, for those who are opposed to Macbeth flee to England to gather their forces for the battle against tyranny. Initially, Easy represents a source of confusion rather than inspiration for the actors. It is only when Cahoot and then the others catch Dogg that Easy becomes part of their play to upstage the tyrannical Inspector.

Malcolm and Macduff discuss the fate of their country while they are in England:

MACDUFF: Bleed, bleed, poor country!
(*Police siren is heard in distance.*)
MALCOLM: It weeps, it bleeds, and each new day a gash
Is added to her wounds. (p. 72)

Stoppard discovers in *Macbeth* a political and contemporary Shakespeare, whom he was reluctant to confront in the earlier plays based around *Hamlet*. The Inspector's second entrance is also incorporated into the performance of the play in such a way as to emphasize political parallels. The siren stops and Malcolm's line about Ross, 'My countryman; but yet I know him not' (p. 72) becomes associated with the Inspector instead. The Inspector's entrance is designed to send the Scots reeling:

Och aye, it's a braw bricht moonlicht nicked, and so are you, you haggis-headed dumbwits, hoots mon ye must think I was born yesterday. (*He drops the accent: to the audience*) – Stay where you are and nobody use the lavatory ...

135

(CAHOOT *enters.*)
Cahoots mon! Where's McLandovsky got himself?   (pp. 72–3)

This brilliant entrance by the music-hall comic is nevertheless almost his
final bow. He is unable to recover this kind of fluency and facility, and
thus power, when confronted by Dogg.

A number of critics find the representation of Dogg as a potentially
subversive language at the end of *Cahoot's Macbeth* to be an unconvinc-
ing one. Although some playwrights might have played up similarities
between an authoritarian prep school and a totalitarian state, Stoppard
emphasizes the differences. Dogg language is based on English and becomes associated with a version of Englishness. It stands for eccentricity,
idiosyncracy and, above all, playfulness. England is a 'dead end' (p. 89)
for Ros and Guil, a country from which no traveller returns. This is an
exception to Stoppard's general rule of standing up for England. It is
probably true that only émigrés like Stoppard himself, or exiles, become
so passionately attached to the eccentricities of both the English language
and people. Mr Moon, Moore and Carr all represent the dignity in both
adversity and obscurity which Stoppard finds to be quintessentially English. This quality is associated very firmly with childhood. Like Ros and
Guil, these other characters derive their strengths as well as their weaknesses from their innocent, childlike view of the world. Mr Moon and
Moore, who do not have children of their own, both play, or want to
play, childish games with their wives. Carr's travesty of history is, as
mentioned, the product of his senility or second childhood. Stoppard is
not offering a version of Englishness in which everything is won or lost
on school playing-fields. He proposes instead a version of it which is
related to what Thomas Whitaker has called 'fields of play'. Mr Dogg's
school, like Albion House in Bennett's *Forty Years On*, symbolizes an
England which cherishes the fun of games. The sportsmen may interrupt
the performance of the historical pageant in *Forty Years On* with their
rugby songs, but they are not part of it. Their supposedly adult humour
may be related to some extent to the Inspector's music-hall act. His gags
are not as blue as Max Miller's, but he would still not be booked for a
childrens' party. Critics who underestimate the strength of Stoppard's
attachment to childhood, and his belief that this is both positive and
creative, will inevitably have difficulties with the fact that Dogg language
is offered as a solution to serious problems. Playwrights like Osborne in
Look Back in Anger and Simon Gray in *Butley* (1971) ultimately represent
a language of childhood, more specifically nursery talk, as being a private

retreat from a complex public reality. There are times when such an interpretation fits Ros and Guil's language and behaviour in *Rosencrantz*. The position in *Dogg's Hamlet, Cahoot's Macbeth* is a more complicated one. Dogg language, which represents all that is positive about both Englishness and childishness, provides a basis for attack as well as for defence.

Cahoot's attempts to use Shakespearian English as a coded, subversive language fail. He likens the Inspector to Macbeth only to find that he is still feeding lines to a domineering comic:

CAHOOT:　'Thou hast it now: King, Cawdor, Glamis, all
　　　　　　As the weird sisters promised . . .'
INSPECTOR:　Kindly leave my wife's family out of this.　　　(p. 61)

The only thing that is bigger than this comedian's mother-in-law, or perhaps it should be sister-in-law, is his own ego. He flattens everybody with his punch-lines. Yet he, together with Boris and Maurice, is not able to make head or tail of Dogg. He remains immune from its infectious charms because he seeks to abolish not just plays but the whole field of play. He may play, and indeed over-play, his own part but nobody else is allowed to join in. The actors, by contrast, respond to Dogg because they thrive on plays and play. Spectators who have already watched *Dogg's Hamlet* ought to be in a position to take the side of the Dogg speakers against the Inspector.

The performance of *Macbeth* continues in Dogg, which fouls up the Inspector's attempts to record it and use it in evidence. His star turns are replaced by ensemble playing. Authoritarian performance gives way to a more democratic one. The Inspector tries to regain this total control during the final stages of *Macbeth*, just as of course Macbeth himself does. He barks 'Wilco zebra over! . . . Green Charlie Angels 15 out' (p. 76) into his walkie-talkie, revealing that under pressure supposedly normal language sounds just as absurd as Dogg does. His hysteria is indeed no longer menacing if it is translated into Dogg:

Scabs! Stinking slobs – crooks. You're nicked, Jock. Punks make me puke. Kick back, I'll break necks, smack chops, put yobs in padlocks and fix facts.　　(p. 78)

Like the Lady's speech in *Dogg's Hamlet*, this outburst can be translated into a string of platitudes and pleasantries. It is thus applauded by Cahoot and the other actors. They have found a way of challenging the Inspector's language game. He used language to reverse meaning: totalitarianism becomes normality. He is now confronted with a language which, with one of Stoppard's neatest touches, reverses the reversal. This does not mean, however, that the play offers an unambiguous last word. The use of Dogg enables the actors to complete their performance, but the Inspector and his heavies construct a wall across the front of the stage which gradually obscures this event. The construction of languages is not just a game. It is also the site of ideological conflict.

Conclusions

Dogg's Hamlet, Cahoot's Macbeth has never been a theatrically or critically fashionable play. This is a pity as the Inspector remains one of Stoppard's best parts. The question of whether the two halves go together to form a unified whole rather misses the point that Stoppard's plays are frequently constructed out of apparently disparate materials. This sets up the opportunities for his ambushes. *Dogg's Hamlet, Cahoot's Macbeth*, like the other works by Stoppard which have been considered in this third part of the book, provides a number of reminders about how to approach *Rosencrantz*. It plays variations on the same theatrical and metadramatical themes, particularly ones concerned with relationships between actors and spectators. It also emphasizes the point that Stoppard's Shakespearian plays depend for their success on visual as well as verbal humour. Both plays parody particular styles of Shakespearian production. A lot of language has been devoted to Stoppard's language games, not enough to his more explicitly theatrical games. The representation of childhood links together these Shakespearian plays, as indeed it does most of Stoppard's work. The comic climate of *Dogg's Hamlet, Cahoot's Macbeth* is broadly similar to that of *Travesties*: 'frivolous' in the first half and more 'serious' in the second one. As Susan Sontag suggests, camp writings explore the complexities of this relationship between the 'frivolous' and the 'serious'. Stoppard's reading of Shakespeare may change, but he still poses questions about this particular relationship. His seriousness about the frivolities of Dogg language leads him to suggest that it offers a possible solution to political problems. The Inspector appears to be 'frivolous' and yet he is a 'serious' danger. Dogg language appears to be 'frivolous' and yet it is also the means of countering this danger. Stoppard does not provide a last word, here and in his other works, to the question of what is 'frivolous' and what is 'serious' because camp denies that there can ever be one.

Appendix: Stoppard and Samuel Beckett's *Waiting for Godot*

Stoppard's debt to Samuel Beckett's *Waiting for Godot* was noticed by Bryden in the review article which helped to launch *Rosencrantz*. It has also been drawn attention to in most of the subsequent commentaries on Stoppard's play. There has, nevertheless, been a surprising reluctance even to consider the possibility that *Rosencrantz*'s relationship with *Godot* is a parodic one. Such a possibility will be discussed here.

Stoppard pays his own tribute to Beckett at the end of *Jumpers*. Archie triumphantly rounds off his justification for the status quo with the words 'Wham, bam, thank you Sam' (p. 87). He acknowledges that this particular speech is based around some of the paradoxes that Beckett gives to Pozzo in *Godot*. The speech also contains a reference to Saint Augustine's account of the fate of the two thieves who were crucified at the same time as Christ was. Beckett has stressed the importance of the 'shape' of this account:

There is a wonderful sentence in Augustine. I wish I could remember the Latin. It is even finer in Latin than in English. 'Do not despair; one of the thieves was saved. Do not presume; one of the thieves was damned.' That sentence has a wonderful shape. It is the shape that matters.

Augustine offers no last word, or resolution, but only two potentially contradictory propositions set against each other. Such a 'shape' is enhanced by the use of minimal language. The human dilemma is stated simply, but not simplistically, in unemotive terms. The quotation suggests the arbitrary, or shapeless, nature of divine judgement while at the same time shaping this shapelessness into a tightly constructed literary form. Stoppard borrows this kind of structure from Beckett and, particularly in *Rosencrantz*, the minimal language which is an inherent part of it. His later work shows that while retaining Beckett's relish for paradoxes, he is much happier with a more exuberant, excessive language in which to express them.

Godot was originally written in French and first performed in Paris. The literal, and still the best, translation of the French title is 'While Waiting for Godot'. The play was first performed in England in 1955. Martin Esslin suggests that playwrights such as Stoppard and Pinter ought to be seen as 'the children of *Godot*'. He is certainly right to draw attention to the importance of the general influence of *Godot* but, as far as Stoppard is concerned, does not consider it in enough detail. An impression is conveyed that *Rosencrantz* is a play in which Stoppard, the grateful but slightly awestruck child, writes reverentially in the idiom of his literary father. Such a reading remains the dominant one. This is unfortunate since it means that *Rosencrantz* tends to be compared with Beckett on Beckett's own terms. There is no reason to deny Stoppard's reverence for Beckett. They both pattern their dialogues around the structure of Augustine's account of the crucifixion: confident statements followed immediately by a denial of them. Stoppard borrows this structure from Beckett's novels as well as from his plays. There is, nevertheless, every reason to return to the definitions of parody that have already been discussed and to suggest that this undoubted reverence may still be mixed in with a more irreverent attitude. There is a kind of literary competition, which was popularized at one time by the *New Statesman*, in which participants are asked to re-write a particular text in the style of another writer. For instance, Dylan Thomas is given permission to jumble up a Jane Austen plot and Noel Coward is encouraged to add a touch of polish to Pinter's dialogue. Stoppard, a compulsive player of games, is offering an extended version of this practice in *Rosencrantz*. He re-writes Shakespeare in the style of Beckett. It is a game which, initially, involves the substitution of one stereotype, or 'instant character', for another. Tramps such as Vladimir and Estragon became, in the wake of *Godot*'s popularity, stereotypes in the contemporary drama of the late 1950s and early 1960s. Stoppard gets the game under way by allowing these modern theatrical stereotypes to replace Renaissance ones. *Travesties* clashes Wildean comedy with political, or epic, theatre. A broadly similar clash of opposing theatrical styles takes place in *Rosencrantz* between the theatre of Shakespeare and the theatre of Beckett. This becomes part of Stoppard's theatre of theatre.

Ros and Guil are much younger than Beckett's tramps, whose lives are nearly finished. Apart from this, there are striking resemblances between Stoppard's characters and Beckett's ones. The parody depends for its success on this kind of instant recognition, which was easier to achieve in the 1960s than it is today. The sight of a double act passing the time on stage should have immediately reminded the more sophisticated members of Stoppard's audience of *Godot*. Orton suggested, in a very perceptive response to *Rosencrantz* recorded in his diary for 9 April 1967, that Ros and Guil enacted the usual dialogue between two bored people waiting for something to happen and playing games to while away the time.

He noted that this was derived from *Look Back in Anger* as well as from *Godot*. Jimmy and Cliff, like Vladimir and Estragon, have their verbal routines for combating the routine of time passing. *Look Back in Anger* and *Godot* were the most influential plays of the 1950s so, as Orton points out, Ros and Guil's double act should have represented the 'usual' or familiar to at least some members of Stoppard's audience. It was suggested in the introduction to this particular analysis of *Rosencrantz* that Stoppard addresses at least two audiences: one consisting of professional theatre-goers and the other of amateur ones. It was also suggested, following on from this distinction, that the popularity of *Rosencrantz* derived largely from its appeal to this second audience. This was helped by the fact that the professionals did not really understand the status and function of the references to *Godot*. They tended to complain that Stoppard was merely offering a pale imitation of Beckett without being attuned to the possibility that parody was the name of Stoppard's game.

Guil is meant to be instantly recognizable as the Vladimir character. They both have some memory of a past, intellectual pretensions and the ability to nursemaid their companions. Ros is meant to be instantly recognizable as the Estragon character. They are both relatively untouched by the past, concerned primarily with the physical and practical aspects of existence and need to be looked after by their companions. The setting for both plays is the theatre itself but, insofar as naturalistic locations are invoked, they both start beside a road in an otherwise characterless landscape.

Some critics suggest that Vladimir represents the head, while Estragon represents the body. The text partially confirms such a reading: Vladimir has bad breath, whereas Estragon has smelly feet. Other references, for instance to the fact that Estragon may once have been a poet, tend to work against such a neat polarity. It can still be maintained, however, that Vladimir and Estragon represent the fractured, or divided, parts of a single personality. Stoppard gestures towards this theme in *Rosencrantz*, although he is primarily concerned to use it as the basis for jokes about mistaken identity. Beckett's treatment of the split personality is certainly a much more disturbing one. Brassell is therefore right to insist that Stoppard's play contains none of the 'dark echoes' to be found in Beckett's one. Vladimir and Estragon have to crawl back to each other because, when they are awake, they are unable to survive apart. Ros and

Guil may also be dependent upon each other, although theirs is still rather a cosy relationship. Beckett, by contrast, exposes the sado-masochistic qualities of such relationships both in *Godot* and later works such as *Endgame* (1957).

Vladimir and Estragon's vigil for Godot is interrupted by the arrival of Pozzo and his servant Lucky. The master keeps his servant at the end of a rope, but the servant appears to be happy, or at least to think that he is happy, with this sadistic arrangement. Lucky certainly has no time for sympathetic responses to his plight. Pozzo and Lucky, who are also both old men, are locked into a sado-masochistic relationship which they are unable to break. Pozzo may announce that he is on his way to sell Lucky and thus to sever once and for all the exploitative ties between them, although all the signs are that it is much too late to do so. Bryden drew a distinction between Stoppard's 'witty' tone and Beckett's more 'despairing' one. This gets close to the differences between *Rosencrantz* and *Godot*, although it requires qualification. Beckett tends to convey hints, or echoes, of despair, without necessarily being explicitly 'despairing'. Indeed, a number of critics have suggested that his writings are beyond despair in much the same way as the Augustine passage is beyond emotion. Bryden's distinction also does not do justice to Beckett's abilities as a comic writer. Lucky's famous 'think' is, at one level, a comic turn. It is a more extended version of some of Guil's academic speeches. The reactions of the on-stage audience to it initially take comic forms: Vladimir and Estragon play the parts of spectators who gradually lose their patience, while Pozzo tries not to listen to it at all. The 'dark echoes' are nevertheless clearly audible since Pozzo, who is driving Lucky to market, is being driven mad by him. There is, once again, a suggestion that mind and body have become divided. Pozzo represents the body since he is primarily concerned with his own physical comfort, whereas Lucky may represent the power of the mind which all too willingly allows itself to be enslaved. Pozzo and Lucky may therefore be seen as different sides of the same coin, or personality, although Beckett's representation of this psychological state is a more disturbing one than Stoppard's variations on this theme. When Stoppard turns *Hamlet* upside down, he conveniently manages to pour away its disturbing representations of political corruption and sexual manipulation. His treatment of *Godot* is a broadly similar one. He retains elements of it, while at the same time contriving to muffle its 'dark echoes'. Such a version of Beckett is in accordance with Stoppard's particular brand of camp parody in which it is only possible to be serious about the frivolous. This has a bearing on the reception of *Rosencrantz* in the 1960s. It is, as suggested, doubtful that the play's popularity had much to do with the specific nature of its parody of Beckett. Stoppard's sophisticated, or caviar, literary game was too clever for many critics who did not even spot that it was being played. It is therefore more likely that the play's success was the result of the fact that the parody of Beckett fulfilled quite different functions. It introduced ordinary theatre-goers to the theatrical games that were associated with avant-garde theatre, while at the same time protecting them from the disturbing qualities which were also a distinctive feature of this kind of theatre.

Beckett's play appears to offer no last word about Godot's identity and intentions. There is, therefore, no answer to the question of whether Vladimir and Estragon, either individually or collectively, ought to despair or to presume. Their world is an arbitrary and shapeless one. Estragon is regularly beaten up while he sleeps in a ditch, whereas Vladimir escapes this fate. No explanations are offered. Godot appears to conform to this patternless pattern rather than to offer any solution to it. He apparently punishes the boy who looks after the sheep, but not the one who looks after the goats. No explanations are available for this choice of victim, which seems to reverse biblical teachings on the relative merits of sheep and goats. Beckett once claimed that, if he had known the answers to questions about the identity of Godot, he 'would have said so in the play'. Perhaps Godot is God and perhaps he is not. The play has a dense set of theological references, most of which Stoppard is more than happy to pour away, although their presence does not necessarily make it one with a religious message about, say, the disappearance of God. One of the problems with religious interpretations is that they tend to assume a little too easily that Beckett represents the present, as opposed to the past, as being absurd and devoid of meaning. It can be argued, however, that what is absurd in *Godot* is Vladimir and Estragon's residual faith that, ultimately, they will be provided with a sense of direction and purpose. Waiting for explanations is a meaningless activity if there are no explanations to be had. There is thus a way of interpreting *Godot* which suggests that it proposes a liberation from, rather than a return to, a religious way of seeing the world. The old tramps, who are content to wait passively for instructions and believe that they will be punished if they do not do so, may represent the absurdity of the so-called 'ages of faith' rather than that of a secular society. Beckett is in fact posing a more complicated question than the one suggested by this rather crude polarity between the religious and the secular. He dramatizes the need for liberation from religion while at the same time showing the impossibility of such a task. The human relationship with God, or with that which is endowed with godlike qualities, becomes another one of the play's seemingly unbreakable sado-masochistic relationships.

Although Hamlet eventually appears in *Rosencrantz*, he nevertheless fulfils some of the same functions as the absent Godot does in Beckett's play. Ros and Guil, like Estragon and Vladimir, are desperately seeking a sense of direction and purpose. Yet Hamlet intensifies their problems rather than offering any solution to them. His actions appear to them to be arbitrary and therefore ultimately unknowable ones, just as Godot's reported actions heighten a sense of the shapelessness of existence. It may be that *Godot*, while not necessarily denying meanings, nevertheless draws attention to the paradox by which the *quest* for them can become destructive, chaotic and eventually meaningless. Stoppard frames his argument in explicitly theatrical terms: Hamlet the theatrical part, or Hamlet the actor who plays this part, has no solution to the problem of what Ros and Guil are supposed to do on stage. Beckett's theatre also draws attention to its own theatricality and yet it is more willing to allow the theatrical to function as a metaphor for either political or religious representations. Godot is certainly an actor who fails to make an entrance, but perhaps God is as well.

Beckett is playing a game with the audience over Godot's identity. Spectators want solutions to enigmatic puzzles and are therefore going to try to reduce the play to a single meaning. This provides an example of the way in which the quest for meaning becomes meaningless. Beckett's audiences, as well as his characters, want to find a shape which will mould away shapelessness. *Godot* is written in such a way as to, quite self-consciously, leave itself open to almost every kind of interpretation. Its theatrical and critical reception therefore represents an extension of its main theme about the quest for meaning. When characters fall over in a Beckett play, as they all do in the second act of *Godot*, the text invites readings which concentrate on religious attitudes to 'the Fall' as well as ones which concentrate on the theatrical implications of this action. Similarly, the presence of a tree in an otherwise barren landscape draws attention to the artificiality of theatrical representations of nature, but it can also be read symbolically. The tree in *Godot* has been taken as the one in the Garden of Eden as well as the Cross itself. Stoppard's games with his audiences are remarkably secularized ones in comparison. He appropriates *Godot*'s theatricality but wants to have little to do with its theology. *Godot* may be an anti-theological play and yet it is one which is, paradoxically, steeped in theology.

The opening moments of *Godot* suggest that Vladimir and Estragon have been left on stage without a *written* script and so have to improvise a *verbal* one. It seems as though they have been abandoned, or left waiting, by a God-like omniscient author. Robbe-Grillet makes a similar point when he draws attention to the way in which Beckett's characters are self-consciously '*en scène*'. This may be translated as 'on stage' or just as 'being there'. They find themselves accidentally present but not correctly prepared to fill in the empty theatrical spaces. Stoppard takes this important aspect of *Godot*, divests it of any possible theological interpretations and uses it as the basis for his parody in *Rosencrantz*. Like Ros and Guil, Vladimir and Estragon attempt to fill these empty theatrical spaces by improvising conversations, which ultimately turn into conversations about conversation. The double act frequently reminds itself, and its audience, how it is supposed to perform and thus draws attention to the gap that exists between carefully scripted dialogue and this kind of hasty verbal improvisation. This attempt to keep a semblance of a play going, which makes the spectators as well as the actors acutely aware of just 'being there', is interrupted by the arrival of Pozzo and Lucky. Like the Player and the Tragedians in *Rosencrantz*, they appear at first sight to offer the chance of a more conventional theatrical plot. Yet Pozzo, like the Player, quickly undermines expectations of plot or character development. He too appears to be stranded on the stage. He belongs to the world of the conventional, well-made play and yet is denied the support of a script. His language, and more particularly the gestures that accompany it, display a kind of theatricality which is comically out of place in the wasteland, with its minimal language and lack of scenery, inhabited by Vladimir and Estragon. He is almost totally dependent on his props: the worn-out whip, picnic basket, pipe, watch and, ultimately, Lucky himself. He also needs the permission of a script before he can accomplish the simplest action. For instance, he agonizes about how he is going to sit down when there is no written dialogue to tell him to do so. Like so many of Beckett's characters in *Godot* and elsewhere, he has come to a standstill. Estragon eventually puts him out of his misery by improvising a parody version of the kind of stage directions which are often rendered as dialogue in naturalistic drama.

The arrival of Pozzo, like that of the Player, intensifies rather than disperses the concentration on theatricality by bringing different styles of acting into conflict. He is a classical actor who suddenly finds himself having to talk in the vacuum created by the absence of a script. He is obsessed by conventional notions about theatrical timing as well as by time itself. Beckett's representation of Pozzo's theatricality, unlike Stoppard's treatment of the Player, nevertheless also invites and encourages political as well as more purely theatrical interpretations. Pozzo is a member of the ruling class with pots of money and power. The Player is always a player. Pozzo, rather like Osrick in *Hamlet*, is shown to be a hollow man who exploits flourish and gesture to disguise this emptiness. He also makes a fetish of commodities. His props may therefore be seen as part of a wider political argument which draws attention to the ways in which the ruling class structure society in terms of commodity and ownership. Lucky carrying some of Pozzo's treasured possessions at the end of a rope is both a logical extension, and graphic representation, of this ruling class ideology. Beckett's theatricality, like Shakespeare's, raises questions about a theatre of politics as well as ones about a theatre of theatre.

Stoppard's use of an on-stage audience to mimic the reactions of the theatre one ought to be instantly recognizable as a device which is self-consciously modelled on Beckett's theatre. While Pozzo is rummaging for his pipe so that he will be theatrically equipped to deliver important speeches Vladimir and Estragon review the production 'so far':

VLADIMIR: Charming evening we're having.
ESTRAGON: Unforgettable.
VLADIMIR: And it's not over.
ESTRAGON: Apparently not.
VLADIMIR: It's only beginning.
ESTRAGON: It's awful.
VLADIMIR: Worse than the pantomime.
ESTRAGON: The circus.
VLADIMIR: The music-hall.
ESTRAGON: The circus.   (pp. 34–5)

Beckett's double act, like Stoppard's one, uses a shorthand, minimalist language in this parody of audience reactions. Like Guil, Vladimir is quite happy to put forward contradictory positions: the play is both 'charming' and 'worse than pantomime'. Later on Vladimir and Estragon perform a similar kind of routine to pass the time: they start by cursing each other and end up with compliments and gestures of reconciliation. Such performances are obviously close to those of Ros and Guil in *Rosencrantz*. Yet Stoppard's dialogues are invariably prosaic. Beckett's sometimes are, as in the instance quoted, although a number of critics have demonstrated how some of them, such as the 'All the dead voices' sequence at the beginning of the second act (pp. 62–3), are genuinely poetic. Stoppard borrows Beckett's language but is not able to use it as effectively.

Vladimir and Estragon are cast as the on-stage audience for Pozzo's speech on 'evening'. It is a very stagey one which, although it has only been an attempt to pass the time by talking about the weather, is nevertheless full of significant gestures and pauses. He then asks the tramps to review this self-conscious performance: 'How did you find me? Good? Fair? Middling? Poor? Positively bad?' (p. 38). Vladimir and Estragon go through the motions of supplying a favourable review. Pozzo is an insecure, vain actor who is totally dependent on audience appreciation. He is also a member of the ruling class who is given leave, or licence, to perform his social role by willing spectators, whose parts are parodied by Vladimir and Estragon. His attempt to dominate the stage raises important questions about relationships between politics and theatre. He therefore has more in common with the Inspector in *Cahoot's Macbeth* than he does with the Player in *Rosencrantz*. He tries to colonize the stage with both his rhetoric and props, which quite literally prop up his authority. It is the loss of these props, perhaps most notably the watch which is a family heirloom also carrying associations with work discipline, which signifies the erosion of this power.

Stoppard's theatre is close to Beckett's one in its employment of various devices, such as the on-stage audience, to remind the spectators of their own roles. Both *Rosencrantz* and *Godot* show their audiences reflections of themselves passing the time and waiting for something more interesting to happen. There is, nevertheless, an important difference of tone as far as relationships with the audience are concerned. This might also be used to suggest that Stoppard is offering a parody of Beckett rather than a more genuine piece of Beckettian drama. *Rosencrantz* is primarily concerned with teasing audiences, whereas *Godot*, despite its use of some of the same techniques, is more concerned with confronting them. Spectators tend not to walk out of *Rosencrantz*, but they left in droves during the first performances of *Godot* in America. The difference can probably be established, at least in shorthand, by considering the physical appearance of the double acts with which audiences are expected to pass the time. Ros and Guil are young, clean-cut and relatively presentable in their somewhat shabby Elizabethan costumes. Apart perhaps from cutting toenails on stage, this pair of likely lads do not have the kind of bad habits to which conventional audiences might object violently. By contrast, Vladimir and Estragon are dirty old men. Estragon has far more basic problems with his feet than Ros does and Vladimir has a weak bladder. He has to leave the stage to relieve himself just before Pozzo's speech on 'evening'. This is turned, through Estragon's running commentary on it, into a joke at the audience's expense, but it is one which is meant to be in bad taste. Stoppard blunts the confrontational edge which is a distinctive part of Beckett's relationship with his audiences. Both plays are, in a general sense, about habits. They illustrate how conversational habits, together with the routines of play, are used to pass the time. The difference is that Stoppard allows his audience to while away the time with a couple of relatively clean characters, whereas Beckett forces his audience to come to terms with, or not, two dirty old men. Beckett's other double act, Pozzo and Lucky, also represents the grotesque rather than the cosy and ever so slightly suburban. Lucky, after all, has running sores on his neck where the rope has chafed him.

Vivian Mercier declared, in what has become a celebrated phrase, that *Godot* is a play in which 'nothing happens, twice'. This is not strictly true: Lucky kicks Estragon, Pozzo loses his watch, Estragon finds a new pair of boots, Pozzo loses his sight and Lucky is struck dumb. The tree has leaves in the second act. Mercier is right, however, to stress that the second act of *Godot* is the same as the first one in terms of its structure. Both of them can be divided into four parts. First of all, the tramps assemble on stage and pass the time either with improvised conversations or else with music-hall routines. Secondly, they are interrupted by the arrival of Pozzo and Lucky. They are quickly drawn into the apparent diversion which these new characters appear to represent in the first act, although in the second one there is more of a sense in which Pozzo and Lucky are seen as an unnecessary disturbance. Beckett is, perhaps, dramatizing the way in which religion, waiting for Godot, can blind people to what is actually happening under their noses. Thirdly, the vacuum that is created by the exit of Pozzo and Lucky is temporarily filled by the arrival of a boy (perhaps the same one both times) with the message that Godot is unable to keep his appointment. Finally the tramps decide to return the next day, which as actors they are bound to do, to resume their vigil for Godot and thus to keep their own appointment. There are also a number of more specific correspondences between the two acts. The structure, or shape, of *Godot* is more successful than that of *Rosencrantz*. *Godot* achieves its own kind of symmetry by appearing to show nothing happening twice. *Rosencrantz* has the additional problem of trying to incorporate *Hamlet* within its structure, which develops into a three act one. Nothing happening three times does not have the same theatrical power as does nothing happening twice. A number of critics have suggested that the inclusion of the third act tends to blur the focus of the play. Orton, who made this criticism, also suggested at a more general level that the attempt to cross Shakespeare with Beckett created other problems. He praised the originality of Stoppard's idea for the play, but thought that it should have

been about the futility of students – always talking, talking, talking and never doing anything. Great events, murders, adulteries, dreadful revenge happening all around them and they just talk.

Stoppard conveys a sense of this kind of futility but is prevented from exploiting its full potential by the inclusion of the parody version of Beckett which demanded minimal language, interspersed with silences, rather than constant chatter. The inclusion both of the third act and the parody of Beckett itself may be taken as examples of the fact that, despite all the affectations of a minimalist position, Stoppard's more excessive kind of drama eventually controls the structure of *Rosencrantz*.

Rosencrantz is close to *Godot* in the way in which it shows actors, and therefore audiences as well, '*en scène*'. Ros and Guil, like Vladimir and Estragon, fill up the empty theatrical spaces by improvising, and then repeating, a number of language games. Both pairs also seize upon other kinds of play in order to pass the time: the attendant lords play with coins while the tramps improvise a routine with their hats. There are also a number of more specific correspondences between the two plays. For instance, Estragon loses his trousers at the end of *Godot* and Ros also inadvertently lets his slip when he takes off his belt during the game of hide and seek with Hamlet. It is, however, more important to stress the differences between the two plays. The pace of the language games may be similar: painful beginnings followed by a brief interlude of intense verbal activity, which is then replaced by silence. Yet there is a much sharper sense in *Godot* that this theatrical rhythm also represents the rhythm of life itself. Stoppard gentles *Godot* in much the same way as he domesticates *Hamlet*. Both *Rosencrantz* and *Godot* are examples of the theatre of theatre and yet Beckett also uses theatricality as a way of posing questions about politics and religion. This heightens the confrontational nature of his dialogue with the audience. Unlike Stoppard, Beckett uses grotesque characters to confront the audience with a reflection of its own (possibly meaningless) quest for meaning. It is therefore dangerous to suggest that Stoppard was one of Beckett's disciples when he wrote *Rosencrantz*. It makes more sense to see the play as an exercise in parody. Stoppard sets his own literary competition, or game, in which *Hamlet* has to be re-written in the style of *Godot*. The fact that Stoppard, anticipating the more complex structure of *Travesties*, parodies Beckett as well as Shakespeare indicates that minimalism was never his favourite theatrical style.

Selected Bibliography

1. Reference Books and Biography

DAVID BRATT *Tom Stoppard: A Reference Guide* (G. K. Hall & Co., 1982)

Modern Drama The annual bibliography, published in the June number, provides the best checklist for recent publications on Stoppard.

MALCOLM PAGE *File on Stoppard* (Methuen, 1986). Strongly recommended. Contains a good selection of critical responses to Stoppard's work as well as detailed bibliographical information.

KENNETH TYNAN 'Withdrawing with Style from the Chaos: Tom Stoppard', in his *Show People: Profiles in Entertainment* (Weidenfeld and Nicolson, 1980), pp. 44–123). The critical commentary can be erratic, but it remains a lively and informative biographical account.

2. Full-length Studies of Stoppard's Plays

C. W. E. BIGSBY *Tom Stoppard* (Longman, 1979 edn)

TIM BRASSELL *Tom Stoppard: An Assessment* (Macmillan, 1985). An important study which contains a good chapter on *Rosencrantz*.

VICTOR L. CAHN *Beyond Absurdity: The Plays of Tom Stoppard* (Fairleigh Dickinson University Press, 1979)

RICHARD CORBALLIS *Stoppard: The Mystery and the Clockwork* (Amber Lane Press, 1984). An interesting interpretation which argues in favour of the unity of Stoppard's dramatic representations and concerns. It also has a very good bibliography.

JOAN FITZPATRICK DEAN *Tom Stoppard: Comedy as a Moral Matrix* (University of Missouri Press, 1981). Recommended.

CHERYL FAROANE 'An Analysis of Tom Stoppard's Plays and Their Productions 1964–1975' (Florida State School of Theatre Ph.D. Thesis, 1980). Offers important insights into Stoppard's theatrical practices through a series of interviews with those involved in particular productions.

LUCINDA PAQUET GABBARD *The Stoppard Plays* (The Whitston Publishing Company, 1982)

Gambit Gambit International Theatre Review, 37: Tom Stoppard Issue (Jonathan Calder Ltd, 1981)

FELICIA HARDISON LONDRÉ *Tom Stoppard* (Ungar, 1981)

RONALD HAYMAN *Tom Stoppard* (Heinemann, 1979 edn). This contains two interviews with Stoppard.

JIM HUNTER *Tom Stoppard's Plays* (Faber and Faber, 1982). Strongly recommended. I found it particularly helpful on performance and comedy.

Critical Studies: Rosencrantz and Guildenstern are Dead

THOMAS R. WHITAKER *Tom Stoppard* (Macmillan, 1983). Recommended.

3. Shorter Studies of Stoppard with Special Reference to *Rosencrantz*: Chapters, Articles and Reviews

WILLIAM BABULA 'The Play-life metaphor in Shakespeare and Stoppard', *Modern Drama*, XV, 1972, pp. 279–81

CLIVE BARKER 'Contemporary Shakespearian Parody in British Theatre', *Shakespeare Jahrbuch*, CV, 1969, pp. 104–20

NORMAN BERLIN '*Rosencrantz and Guildenstern are Dead:* Theater of Criticism', *Modern Drama*, XVI, 1973, pp. 269–77

ROBERT BRUSTEIN 'Waiting for Hamlet' in *The Third Theatre* (Jonathan Cape, 1970)

PETER CARROLL 'They Have Their Entrances and Their Exits: *Rosencrantz and Guildenstern are Dead*', *Teaching of English*, XX, 1971, pp. 50–60

DOUGLAS COLBY 'The Game of Coin Tossing: *Rosencrantz and Guildenstern are Dead*' in *As the Curtain Rises: On Contemporary British Drama 1966–1976* (Fairleigh Dickinson University Press, 1978), pp. 28–45. I found this very helpful.

JOHN WILLIAM COOKE 'The Optical Allusion: Perception and Form in Stoppard's *Travesties*', *Modern Drama*, XXIV, 1981, pp. 525–39. An interesting analysis of Stoppard's use of fragments.

BRIAN CROSSLEY 'An Investigation of Stoppard's "Hound" and "Foot"', *Modern Drama*, XX, 1977, pp. 77–86

MANFRED DRAUDT 'Two Sides of the Same Coin, or the Same Side of Two Coins', *English Studies*, LXII, 1981, pp. 348–57. Contains a number of good observations on actor–spectator relationships.

ROBERT EGAN 'A Thin Beam of Light: The Purpose of Playing in *Rosencrantz and Guildenstern are Dead*', *Theater Journal*, XXXI, 1979, pp. 59–69

G. J. GIANAKARIS 'Absurdism Altered: *Rosencrantz and Guildenstern are Dead*', *Drama Survey*, VII, 1968–9, pp. 52–8. 'Stoppard's Adaptations of Shakespeare: *Dogg's Hamlet, Cahoot's Macbeth*', *Comparative Drama*, XVII, 1984, pp. 22–40

MARGARET GOLD 'Who are the Dadas of *Travesties?*', *Modern Drama*, XXI, 1978, pp. 59–66

WILLIAM E. GRUBER 'Wheels within Wheels, etcetera: Artistic Design in *Rosencrantz and Guildenstern are Dead*', *Comparative Drama*, XV, 1981–2, pp. 291–310

CLIVE JAMES 'Count Zero Splits the Infinite: Tom Stoppard's Plays', *Encounter*, XLV, November 1975, pp. 68–76

HELENE KEYSSAR-FRANKE 'The Strategy of *Rosencrantz and Guildenstern are Dead*', *Educational Theatre Journal*, XXVII, 1975, pp. 85–97. A good exploration of audience responses to Stoppard's theatricality.

JILL L. LEVENSON '*Hamlet* Andante/*Hamlet* Allegro: Tom Stoppard's Two Versions', *Shakespeare Survey*, XXVI, 1983, pp. 21–8

152

PHILIP ROBERTS 'Tom Stoppard: Serious Artist or Siren?', *Critical Quarterly*, XX, 1978, pp. 84–92

DAVID K. ROD 'Carr's Views on Art and Politics in Tom Stoppard's *Travesties*', *Modern Drama*, XXVI, 1983, pp. 536–42

JUNE SCHLUETER 'Stoppard's Moon and Birdboot, Rosencrantz and Guildenstern' in *Metafictional Characters in Modern Drama* (Columbia University Press, 1979), pp. 89–103

JOHN RUSSELL TAYLOR 'The Road to Dusty Death', *Plays and Players*, July 1967, pp. 12–15

IRVING WARDLE 'A Grin without a Cat', *The Times*, 22 June 1968

THOMAS R. WHITAKER 'Playing the Player' in *Fields of Play in Modern Drama* (Princeton University Press, 1977), pp. 9–34

ROBERT WILCHER 'Tom Stoppard and the Art of Communication', *Journal of Beckett Studies*, VIII, 1982, pp. 105–23

4. Contemporary Drama

MALCOLM BRADBURY AND DAVID PALMER (eds) *Contemporary English Drama* (Edward Arnold, 1981). Recommended. Contains a contribution by Ruby Cohn on 'Tom Stoppard: Light Drama and Dirges in Marriage', pp. 109–20

JOHN ELSOM *Post-War British Theatre* (Routledge and Kegan Paul, 1976)

RONALD HAYMAN *British Theatre since 1945* (Oxford University Press, 1979). *Theatre and Anti-Theatre: New Movements since Beckett* (Secker and Warburg, 1979). Includes an analysis of Stoppard but is also recommended as an important general analysis and survey.

ALAN SINFIELD (ed.) *Society and Literature 1945–1970* (Methuen, 1983). Especially Sinfield's own contribution on 'The Theatre and its Audiences', pp. 173–97.

JOHN RUSSELL TAYLOR *Anger and After: A Guide to the New British Drama* (Penguin, 1963). *The Second Wave: British Drama of the Sixties* (Methuen, 1978 edn). Contains a short chapter on Stoppard.

SIMON TRUSSLER (ed.) *New Theatre Voices of the Seventies: Sixteen Interviews from Theatre Quarterly* (Eyre Methuen, 1981). Reprints the important interview 'Ambushes for the Audience'.

5. Parody, Camp and Postmodernism: Theories and Practices

ALAN BENNETT *Forty Years On and other plays* (Faber and Faber, 1985)

SIMON BRETT (ed.) *The Faber Book of Parodies* (Faber, 1984). This contains Richard Curtis's 'The Skinhead Hamlet', pp. 316–20

ITALO CALVINO *If on a Winter's Night a Traveller* (Picador, 1982)

TIM DOWLEY (ed.) *Taking off: An Anthology of Parodies, Send-ups and Imitations* (Methuen, 1984)

Critical Studies: Rosencrantz and Guildenstern are Dead

HAL FOSTER (ed.) *Postmodern Culture* (Pluto Press, 1985). Contains Frederic Jameson's essay on 'Postmodernism and Consumer Society', pp. 11–25.

JOHN FOWLES *The French Lieutenant's Woman* (Jonathan Cape, 1969)

JOHN FLETCHER *Alain Robbe-Grillet* (Methuen, 1983)

MICHAEL FRAYN *Plays: One* (Methuen, 1985)

GRAEME GARDEN AND BILL ODDIE *I'm Sorry I'll Read That Again: The Classic Scripts* (Javelin Books, 1985)

RONALD HARWOOD *The Dresser* (Amber Lane Press, 1980)

LINDA HUTCHEON *A Theory of Parody: The Teachings of Twentieth-Century Art Forms* (Methuen, 1985). This contains a brief reference to Stoppard, but nevertheless sets out a context in which his work needs to be considered.

DAVID LODGE *The British Museum is Falling Down* (Macgibbon & Kee, 1965)

RICHARD O'BRIEN *The Rocky Horror Show* (Samuel French, 1983)

JOE ORTON *Loot* (Methuen, 1967). *What the Butler Saw* (Methuen, 1969)

E. O. PARROTT (ed.) *Imitations of Immortality: A Book of Literary Parodies* (Viking, 1986)

MICHAEL PALIN AND TERRY JONES *Ripping Yarns* (Eyre Methuen, 1978)

MARGARET A. ROSE *Parody/Metafiction: An Analysis of Parody as a Critical Mirror to the Writing and Reception of Fiction* (Croom Helm, 1979). Offers a concise and perceptive reading of *Travesties* (pp. 74–6), as well as suggesting the basis for a comparison between Fellini and Stoppard.

SUSAN SONTAG 'Notes on "Camp"', *Against Interpretation* (Farrar, Straus & Giroux, 1966), pp. 275–92. I found this invaluable.

JOHN O. THOMPSON (ed.) *Monty Python: Complete and Utter Theory of the Grotesque* (BFI Publishing, 1982). I have not used material from this collection, although I would recommend it to anyone wanting to do more detailed work on thematic connections between Stoppard and *Python*. Stoppard's collaboration with Terry Gilliam on the filmscript for *Brazil* (1985) might also be worth considering in this context.

ROGER WILMUT *From Fringe to Flying Circus: Celebrating a Unique Generation of Comedy 1960–1980* (Methuen, 1982 edn)

6. Some Criticism on *Hamlet*

NIGEL ALEXANDER *Poison, Play and Duel* (Routledge and Kegan Paul, 1971)

ANNE BARTON 'Introduction', *Hamlet* (New Penguin Shakespeare, 1980), pp. 5–57. Strongly recommended.

DAVID BEVINGTON (ed.) *Twentieth-Century Interpretations of Hamlet: A Collection of Critical Essays* (Prentice-Hall Inc., 1968). This contains Maynard Mack's important essay on 'The World of *Hamlet*', pp. 47–63.

PETER DAVISON *Hamlet: Text and Performance* (Macmillan, 1983)

ALAN C. DESSEN *Elizabethan Stage Conventions and Modern Interpretations* (Cambridge University Press, 1984)

R. A. FOAKES '*Hamlet* and the Court of Elsinore', *Shakespeare Survey*, 9, pp. 35–43. Recommended.

STEPHEN GREENBLATT *Renaissance Self-fashioning from More to Shakespeare* (University of Chicago Press, 1980). Although this does not deal with *Hamlet*, I found its analysis of improvisation particularly useful for my own reading of the play.

LISA JARDINE *Still Harping on Daughters: Women and Drama in the Age of Shakespeare* (Harvester Press, 1983)

JOHN JUMP (ed.) *Shakespeare: Hamlet* (Macmillan Casebook, 1968). A useful collection but it needs to be brought up to date.

ALVIN B. KERNAN *The Playwright as Magician: Shakespeare's Image of the Poet in the English Public Theater* (Yale University Press, 1979). This contains a good chapter on theatricality in *Hamlet*.

JACQUES LACAN 'Desire and the Interpretation of Desire in *Hamlet*' in S. Felman (ed.) *Literature and Psychoanalysis* (Johns Hopkins University Press, 1982), pp. 11–52

HARRY LEVIN *The Question of Hamlet* (Oxford University Press, 1959). Remains one of the best interpretations of the play.

KENNETH MUIR AND STANLEY WELLS (eds) *Aspects of Hamlet* (Cambridge University Press, 1979)

PATRICIA PARKER AND GEOFFREY HARTMAN (eds) *Shakespeare and the Question of Theory* (Methuen, 1985). I found the essays by Terence Hawkes and Elaine Showalter particularly useful.

ELEANOR PROSSER *Hamlet and Revenge* (Stanford University Press, 1967)

ANNE RIGHTER *Shakespeare and the Idea of the Play* (Chatto and Windus, 1962)

REBECCA SMITH 'A Heart Cleft in Twain: The Dilemma of Shakespeare's Gertrude' in Caroline Lenz *et al* (eds), *The Woman's Part: Feminist Criticism of Shakespeare* (University of Illinois Press, 1980), pp. 194–210

JOHN DOVER WILSON *What Happens in Hamlet* (Cambridge University Press, 1937 edn)

7. *Rosencrantz and Guildenstern are Dead* and *Waiting For Godot*

A number of the works already cited discuss Stoppard's relationship with Beckett. In addition to them, and to the various studies of Beckett by both Ruby Cohn and John Fletcher, I consulted the following accounts:

MARTIN ESSLIN *The Theatre of the Absurd* (Penguin, 1968 edn)

AXEL KRUSE 'Tragicomedy and Tragic Burlesque: *Waiting for Godot* and *Rosencrantz and Guildenstern are Dead*', *Sydney Studies in English*, I, 1978–9, pp. 76–96

BERT. O. STATES *The Shape of Paradox: An Essay on Waiting for Godot* (University of California Press, 1978). Recommended.

ROBERT WILCHER 'The Museum of Tragedy: *Endgame* and *Rosencrantz and Guildenstern are Dead*', *Journal of Beckett Studies*, IV, 1979, pp. 43–54
The quotations from Orton's Diaries in the Appendix are taken from John Lahr (ed.), *The Orton Diaries* (Methuen, 1986)

8. Modern Shakespeare Stage Adaptations

I did not, unfortunately, have room to deal with stage adaptations of Shakespeare by some of Stoppard's contemporaries. Charles Marowitz's work offers an interesting contrast to Stoppard's Shakespeare plays, so *The Marowitz Shakespeare: Adaptations and Collages from Hamlet, Macbeth, The Taming of the Shrew, Measure for Measure and The Merchant of Venice* (Marion Boyars, 1978) is recommended. It would be interesting to contrast Edward Bond's political *Lear* (Eyre Methuen, 1974) with Stoppard's various versions of *Hamlet*. Ruby Cohn's *Modern Shakespeare Offshoots* (Princeton University Press, 1976) is recommended to those who want to pursue this and other related themes.

9. Additional Material

I did not consult the following books or articles, most of which were published after I had completed my own work. They should nevertheless still be listed for the benefit of students.

MICHAEL BILLINGTON *Stoppard the Playwright* (Methuen, 1987). Contains a good analysis of *Malquist*.

ELIN DIAMOND 'Stoppard's *Dogg's Hamlet, Cahoot's Macbeth*: The Uses of Shakespeare', *Modern Drama*, XXIX, 1986, pp. 593–600

RICHARD DUTTON *Modern Tragicomedy and the British Tradition* (Oklahoma University Press, 1986)

ANTHONY JENKINS *The Theatre of Tom Stoppard* (Cambridge University Press, 1987)

JOHN M. PERLETTE 'Theatre at the Limit: *Rosencrantz and Guildenstern are Dead*', *Modern Drama*, XXVIII, 1986, pp. 659–69

SUSAN RUSINKO *Tom Stoppard* (Twayne Publishers, 1986)

NEIL SAMMELLS 'Earning Liberties: *Travesties* and *The Importance of Being Earnest*', *Modern Drama*, XXIX, pp. 376–87

RODNEY SIMARD *Postmodern Drama: Contemporary Playwrights in America and Britain* (University Press of America, 1984). Chapter Four is on Stoppard.

FOR THE BEST IN PAPERBACKS, LOOK FOR THE 🐧

In every corner of the world, on every subject under the sun, Penguin represents quality and variety – the very best in publishing today.

For complete information about books available from Penguin – including Pelicans, Puffins, Peregrines and Penguin Classics – and how to order them, write to us at the appropriate address below. Please note that for copyright reasons the selection of books varies from country to country.

In the United Kingdom: For a complete list of books available from Penguin in the U.K., please write to *Dept E.P., Penguin Books Ltd, Harmondsworth, Middlesex, UB7 0DA*

In the United States: For a complete list of books available from Penguin in the U.S., please write to *Dept BA, Penguin, 299 Murray Hill Parkway, East Rutherford, New Jersey 07073*

In Canada: For a complete list of books available from Penguin in Canada, please write to *Penguin Books Canada Ltd, 2801 John Street, Markham, Ontario L3R 1B4*

In Australia: For a complete list of books available from Penguin in Australia, please write to the *Marketing Department, Penguin Books Australia Ltd, P.O. Box 257, Ringwood, Victoria 3134*

In New Zealand: For a complete list of books available from Penguin in New Zealand, please write to the *Marketing Department, Penguin Books (NZ) Ltd, Private Bag, Takapuna, Auckland 9*

In India: For a complete list of books available from Penguin, please write to *Penguin Overseas Ltd, 706 Eros Apartments, 56 Nehru Place, New Delhi, 110019*

In Holland: For a complete list of books available from Penguin in Holland, please write to *Penguin Books Nederland B.V., Postbus 195, NL–1380AD Weesp, Netherlands*

In Germany: For a complete list of books available from Penguin, please write to *Penguin Books Ltd, Friedrichstrasse 10 – 12, D–6000 Frankfurt Main 1, Federal Republic of Germany*

In Spain: For a complete list of books available from Penguin in Spain, please write to *Longman Penguin España, Calle San Nicolas 15, E–28013 Madrid, Spain*

FOR THE BEST IN PAPERBACKS, LOOK FOR THE 🐧

PENGUIN CLASSICS

Netochka Nezvanova   Fyodor Dostoyevsky

Dostoyevsky's first book tells the story of 'Nameless Nobody' and introduces many of the themes and issues which will dominate his great masterpieces.

Selections from the Carmina Burana   A verse translation by David Parlett

The famous songs from the *Carmina Burana* (made into an oratorio by Carl Orff) tell of lecherous monks and corrupt clerics, drinkers and gamblers, and the fleeting pleasures of youth.

Fear and Trembling   Søren Kierkegaard

A profound meditation on the nature of faith and submission to God's will which examines with startling originality the story of Abraham and Isaac.

Selected Prose   Charles Lamb

Lamb's famous essays (under the strange pseudonym of Elia) on anything and everything have long been celebrated for their apparently innocent charm; this major new edition allows readers to discover the darker and more interesting aspects of Lamb.

The Picture of Dorian Gray   Oscar Wilde

Wilde's superb and macabre novella, one of his supreme works, is reprinted here with a masterly Introduction and valuable Notes by Peter Ackroyd.

A Treatise of Human Nature   David Hume

A universally acknowledged masterpiece by 'the greatest of all British Philosophers' – A. J. Ayer

FOR THE BEST IN PAPERBACKS, LOOK FOR THE 🐧

PENGUIN CLASSICS

A Passage to India E. M. Forster

Centred on the unresolved mystery in the Marabar Caves, Forster's great work provides the definitive evocation of the British Raj.

The Republic Plato

The best-known of Plato's dialogues, *The Republic* is also one of the supreme masterpieces of Western philosophy whose influence cannot be overestimated.

The Life of Johnson James Boswell

Perhaps the finest 'life' ever written, Boswell's *Johnson* captures for all time one of the most colourful and talented figures in English literary history.

Remembrance of Things Past (3 volumes) Marcel Proust

This revised version by Terence Kilmartin of C. K. Scott Moncrieff's original translation has been universally acclaimed – available for the first time in paperback.

Metamorphoses Ovid

A golden treasury of myths and legends which has proved a major influence on Western literature.

A Nietzsche Reader Friedrich Nietzsche

A superb selection from all the major works of one of the greatest thinkers and writers in world literature, translated into clear, modern English.

FOR THE BEST IN PAPERBACKS, LOOK FOR THE 🐧

PENGUIN CLASSICS

FOR THE BEST IN PAPERBACKS, LOOK FOR THE 🐧

PENGUIN CLASSICS

Benjamin Disraeli	**Sybil**
George Eliot	**Adam Bede**
	Daniel Deronda
	Felix Holt
	Middlemarch
	The Mill on the Floss
	Romola
	Scenes of Clerical Life
	Silas Marner
Elizabeth Gaskell	**Cranford** and **Cousin Phillis**
	The Life of Charlotte Brontë
	Mary Barton
	North and South
	Wives and Daughters
Edward Gibbon	**The Decline and Fall of the Roman Empire**
George Gissing	**New Grub Street**
Edmund Gosse	**Father and Son**
Richard Jefferies	**Landscape with Figures**
Thomas Macaulay	**The History of England**
Henry Mayhew	**Selections from London Labour** and **The London Poor**
John Stuart Mill	**On Liberty**
William Morris	**News from Nowhere** and **Selected Writings and Designs**
Walter Pater	**Marius the Epicurean**
John Ruskin	**'Unto This Last' and Other Writings**
Sir Walter Scott	**Ivanhoe**
Robert Louis Stevenson	**Dr Jekyll and Mr Hyde**
William Makepeace Thackeray	**The History of Henry Esmond**
	Vanity Fair
Anthony Trollope	**Barchester Towers**
	Framley Parsonage

FOR THE BEST IN PAPERBACKS, LOOK FOR THE 🐧

PENGUIN CLASSICS

FOR THE BEST IN PAPERBACKS, LOOK FOR THE 🐧

PLAYS IN PENGUIN

Edward Albee   **Who's Afraid of Virginia Woolf?**

Alan Ayckbourn   **The Norman Conquests**

Bertolt Brecht   **Parables for the Theatre (The Good Woman of Setzuan/The Caucasian Chalk Circle)**

Anton Chekhov   **Plays (The Cherry Orchard/The Three Sisters/Ivanov/The Seagull/Uncle Vanya)**

Michael Hastings   **Tom and Viv**

Henrik Ibsen   **Hedda Gabler/Pillars of Society/The Wild Duck**

Eugène Ionesco   **Absurd Drama (Rhinoceros/The Chair/The Lesson)**

Ben Jonson   **Three Comedies (Volpone/The Alchemist/Bartholomew Fair)**

D. H. Lawrence   **Three Plays (The Collier's Friday Night/The Daughter-in-Law/The Widowing of Mrs Holroyd)**

Arthur Miller   **Death of a Salesman**

John Mortimer   **A Voyage Round My Father/What Shall We Tell Caroline?/The Dock Brief**

J. B. Priestley   **Time and the Conways/I Have Been Here Before/An Inspector Calls/The Linden Tree**

Peter Shaffer   **Amadeus**

Bernard Shaw   **Plays Pleasant (Arms and the Man/Candida/The Man of Destiny/You Never Can Tell)**

Sophocles   **Three Theban Plays (Oedipus the King/Antigone/Oedipus at Colonus)**

Arnold Wesker   **The Wesker Trilogy (Chicken Soup with Barley/Roots/I'm Talking about Jerusalem)**

Oscar Wilde   **Plays (Lady Windermere's Fan/A Woman of No Importance/An Ideal Husband/The Importance of Being Earnest/Salome)**

Thornton Wilder   **Our Town/The Skin of Our Teeth/The Matchmaker**

Tennessee Williams   **Sweet Bird of Youth/A Streetcar Named Desire/The Glass Menagerie**

FOR THE BEST IN PAPERBACKS, LOOK FOR THE 🐧

PENGUIN MASTERSTUDIES AND CRITICAL STUDIES

This comprehensive list, designed for advanced level and first-year under-graduate studies, includes:

SUBJECTS
Applied Mathematics
Biology
Drama: Text into Performance
Geography
Pure Mathematics

LITERATURE
Absalom and Achitophel
Barchester Towers
Dr Faustus
Eugénie Grandet
The Great Gatsby
Gulliver's Travels
Joseph Andrews
The Mill on the Floss
A Passage to India
Persuasion *and* Emma
Portrait of a Lady
Tender Is the Night
Vanity Fair
The Waste Land

CHAUCER
The Knight's Tale
The Miller's Tale
The Nun's Priest's Tale
The Pardoner's Tale
The Prologue to The Canterbury
    Tales
A Chaucer Handbook

SHAKESPEARE
Antony & Cleopatra
Hamlet
King Lear
Measure for Measure
Much Ado About Nothing
Othello
The Tempest
A Shakespeare Handbook